D1622860

**the simple guide to**

## Choosing, Training &

# RAISING A DOG

*Richard G. Beauchamp*

**t.f.h.**

T.F.H. Publications, Inc.

# Contents

*AKC Breeds page 15–21*

Pads or Papers? page 67

Dog
Foods
page 139

*Older Dogs and Exercise page 149*

*Vaccination Schedule page 170*

# Part One
# Choosing Your Dog

"So, this means I'm not getting a little brother, doesn't it."

# Your New Family Member

Whether your new dog has already taken up residence in your home or you are still thinking about dog ownership, your purchase of a family dog indicates that you plan to become a responsible dog owner. "Responsibility" is a key word that will be emphasized throughout this book.

Dogs are living, breathing, totally dependent creatures. Their safety and well-being lie entirely in our hands. Unfortunately, there are far too many irresponsible people who enter into dog ownership as though they were buying a magazine or some disposable toy.

If dogs could talk, I can only wonder what the thousands of abandoned dogs in animal shelters across the country would say to us. There is no

A Lab puppy would be a welcome addition to any household.

*Try to choose a dog that will best suit your lifestyle.*

**Did You Know?**
Many rescue organizations hold Adoption Days at local pet stores on weekends. The animals are presented by rescue volunteers who, in many cases, have taken the time to observe the dogs' personalities and reactions to situations. Many lovely, stable dogs, both purebred and mixed breed, are available on these special days.

doubt that they would have some profound comments on how well we have fulfilled our part of the relationship with man's best friend.

The thought of dog ownership gives most people a warm, fuzzy feeling. What better image could there be than good old Shep sitting faithfully at the door each evening, waiting to lavish unlimited adoration on you when you come home, or the thought of a rolly-polly puppy taking a quiet little snooze on your lap. Appealing? Certainly. And all of these wonderful scenarios are part of dog ownership. However, let me caution you that these touching images are but a small part of the big picture.

All puppies are cuddly and cute, but they are also very adventurous and mischievous little creatures. At the same time, they are entirely dependent upon their human owners for everything once they leave their mother and littermates. Furthermore, the innocent-looking and dependent little puppy quickly becomes a dynamo of energy with adolescent hormones that continuously rage and inspire relentless activity.

Your adult dog will adore you and strive to please you, but you must teach him what is and is not acceptable. It is highly unlikely that you will be bringing a totally trained adult dog home with you, and even if you were to do so, what will he be trained to do? Will the dog be trained to accommodate your household and lifestyle? There are many things to consider before dashing off to the shopping mall for toothpaste and returning with a new puppy instead. Bringing home a dog without seriously considering the commitment involved can be a serious mistake. The prospective dog owner must clearly understand the amount of time, work, and patience involved in the ownership of any pet. Failure to understand the extent of this commitment is one of the primary reasons so many unwanted canines end their lives in animal shelters.

There is a fundamental question that must precede all others when it comes to making the decision to own a dog. That question is: Does the person who will ultimately be responsible for the dog's care and well-being actually want a dog? If the answer is anything less than a firm "Yes," stop there. Perhaps you should consider a goldfish or hamster instead. If the prospective dog owner lives alone, the only thing necessary is a strong desire to make the commitment that dog ownership entails. In the case of family households, however, it becomes a situation that should be discussed among all the members.

These buddies take time out for some puppy love.

In the average household, mothers–even working mothers–are most often given the additional responsibility of caring for the family pet, which includes feeding, grooming, and veterinary care.

Although pets are a wonderful method of teaching children responsibility, it should be remembered that the enthusiasm that inspires children to promise anything in order to have a new puppy may quickly wane. Who will take care of the puppy once the novelty wears off, and does that person actually want the responsibility of caring for a pet?

The desire to own a dog aside, does the prospective family's lifestyle allow for responsible dog ownership? If the entire family is away from home from early morning to late at night, who will provide for all of a puppy's needs? Neccessities like feeding, exercise, outdoor access, and so on cannot be provided if no one is home.

## The Right Fit

Another important factor to consider is what type of dog would be suitable for your household. There are hundreds of breeds of dog and more combinations of breeds than there are stars in the sky. Dogs the size of Lassie and Rin Tin Tin project images of heroism and safety to many people. Their bravery goes without saying, but will a tiny apartment in the middle of a big city be suitable for these larger dogs? Anything is possible, but be aware of the amount of work that is entailed in providing a dog of that size with adequate time and exercise.

Small or large, furry or smooth, all dogs make lovable friends.

An energetic Lab is the perfect companion to take on a jog.

Small or large breeds, smooth-coated or long-haired dogs—the possibilities are endless. Some breeds can handle the rough and tumble play of young children; some cannot. On the other hand, some dogs are so large and clumsy, especially as puppies, that they could easily and unintentionally injure an infant. There is also the matter of grooming. A luxuriously coated dog is certainly beautiful to behold, but maintaining all of that hair takes time. It should be understood that short-haired dogs also shed their coats in the home; longer hair may be more noticeable, but short hair can be extremely difficult to pick up.

Despite any particular breed's intelligence and trainability, it should be understood that a new dog must be taught every household rule which he is to observe. No dog can be expected to know all the rules you have set down for him on arrival. Some dogs catch on more quickly than others, but puppies are just as inclined to forget or disregard lessons as are young human children.

A person who wants a dog to go along on morning jogs or long distance runs is not going to be particularly happy with a lethargic or short-legged breed. Neither is the fastidious housekeeper, whose picture of the ideal dog is one that lies quietly at the feet of his master by the hour and never sheds, going to be particularly happy with the shaggy dog whose temperament is reminiscent of a hurricane.

Parents love their children, no matter what they look like. Unfortunately, this does not always apply equally to our pets, particularly because so many people look at dogs as disposable property. "We are moving," "I'm allergic," "Too destructive," "Too big,"

## Who Should Own a Dog?

The following list of questions should be answered by everyone who is contemplating the addition of a dog to their household. Anything other than affirmative answers would indicate that serious consideration should be given before a final decision is made to bring a dog home.

1. Does everyone in the household want a dog?

2. Is the person who will be responsible for the dog's day-to-day care (including exercise) willing and able to do so?

3. Does the lifestyle and schedule of the household lend itself to the demands of proper dog care?

4. Is the type of dog being considered suitable for the individual or the household?

5. If there are children in the home, are they old enough to understand what proper treatment of a dog entails?

6. Are the children old enough to be able to withstand the enthusiasm of an excitable dog?

"Too small"–these are just a few of the reasons that are given to animal shelter volunteers when people decide to give up their dogs. In actual fact, these "reasons" are just excuses to cover up the fact that the dog didn't live up to the buyer's dog/owner fantasy.

There's no doubt that all puppies are cute. However, not all puppies grow up to be particularly attractive adults, or at least not what some of us may consider attractive. What is considered beautiful by one person may not necessarily be seen as remotely attractive by another. Even if the puppy or dog you are considering is exactly what you feel your ideal dog should look like, please understand that you will not be living with a picture of that dog, but a living, breathing, dependent animal.

This floppy-eared Beagle puppy could capture anyone's heart.

Purebred puppies will usually look very similar to their parents.

It is also important to understand that as far as dogs are concerned, what you see now may be far from what you may get as the youngster begins to mature. That floppy-eared, forlorn little pup could turn out to be hell on wheels. The tall, intelligent-looking aristocrat could easily turn out to be somewhat of a dunce in the learning department. Far too many people select their dogs based on appearances alone. They give no consideration whatsoever to how the dog's personality will mesh with theirs.

Size and temperament can vary to a degree, even with purebred dogs. Nevertheless, selective breeding over many generations has produced dogs that give the would-be owner a reasonable assurance of what the purebred puppy will look and act like as an adult. Points of attractiveness completely aside, this predictability is more important than one might think.

In the year 2000, the American Kennel Club (AKC) recognized 148 breeds of dog. Primarily based on original purpose, the AKC has categorized the breeds into seven groups: the Sporting, Hound, Working, Herding, Terrier, Toy, and Non-Sporting Groups.

## The Purebred Dog

Purebred puppies will grow up to look like their adult relatives and, by and large, they will behave much like the rest of their family. Any dog has the potential to be a loving companion. However, if chosen correctly, a purebred dog offers some assurance that he will not only suit the owner's personality, but his aesthetic demands as well.

This can be of consequence to the potential dog owner, so let us take a brief look at the great variety of dogs there are and what their ownership might entail in the way of companionship and management.

## Sporting Breeds

This group includes most of the hunting dogs–pointers, retrievers, setters, and spaniels. Their sizes range from small (Cocker Spaniel) to large (the setters and retrievers). The dogs in this group are usually happy-go-lucky, people-loving, and very trainable. They are seldom aggressive, but they do need plenty of training and a great deal of exercise.

## Hound Breeds

There are two basic subdivisions in this group–sighthounds (such as Afghan Hounds, Whippets, and Greyhounds) and scenthounds (such as Beagles, Basset Hounds, and Bloodhounds). Their manner of performance in the field is indicated by their names. Sighthounds are relatively placid dogs that are inclined to be quite aloof with strangers and are definitely not to be trusted if fluffy little things go scurrying by. Scenthounds are the good old boys of the canine world. Laid back, they get on well with the entire world. However, scenthounds are inclined to be a bit on the stubborn side and can wander to follow interesting smells, wherever those smells may take them.

## Working Breeds

Most dogs in this group are what would be considered large or giant breeds (such as Rottweilers, Great Danes, St. Bernards). Happiest when given a job to do, working dogs are extremely intelligent and thrive on training. In most cases, they are protective and territorial.

Labrador Retriever

Newfoundland

Part 1

### Terrier Breeds

Terriers fall into three general classifications: short-legged (such as Scottish Terriers), long-legged (such as Wire Fox Terriers or Airedale Terriers), and the bull-and-terrier breeds (such as English Bull Terriers and Staffordshire Bull Terriers). Most of the terriers have hair-trigger responses, and although great with people, it doesn't take much to get them to respond to a challenge from another dog.

### Toy Breeds

These are the little guys–Chihuahuas, Pekingese, and Toy Poodles. The diminutive Toys love their owners and live to be with them. They have lots of zip and give voice to most everything they see and do.

### Non-Sporting Breeds

This is the AKC's catch-all group. Chinese Shar-Peis, American Eskimo Dogs, and Poodles all call this group their home. Because they originate from all different kinds of backgrounds and ancestries, it is impossible to characterize them as a group.

Pug

### Herding Breeds

As their name implies, these fellows were bred to work livestock. From the tall (Bouvier des Flandres) to the short (Welsh Corgis), herding dogs must be given a job to do–whether it's obedience training, playing Frisbee™, or bringing in the morning newspaper. The herders have all the drive in the world, so life as a couch potato or being confined to a small room day in and day out could easily make them neurotic.

There are many books available through your pet outlet or bookstore devoted to the specific breed groups and the dogs within the groups that can give you greater detail on each breed and its special needs.

### Mixed Breeds

Mixed breeds are simply an amalgamation of two or more of any of the purebred breeds. The same genes that dictate the characteristics of a purebred exist in the genetic makeup of the mixed breed; however, the genes from one ancestor may serve to tone down or obliterate a characteristic from another ancestor. As a result, black becomes gray, and the all-out extrovert becomes relatively settled down. You might even get a dog that looks like a terrier in the body of a hound and acts like a working dog. Until the mixed breed matures from puppyhood, it is often hard to tell exactly what an individual dog may look like or how he will behave. Certainly, this makes little difference to a person who is simply interested in companionship and is willing to put up with the personality of any dog that is able to put up with theirs.

There are a huge number of homeless mixed-breed dogs (and purebreds, for that matter) of all ages that would leap at the opportunity to be adopted and live the rest of their lives as a member of someone's family. Responsible rescue organizations all over the country specialize in rehoming dogs. Some of these volunteer organizations make it a practice to track down as much of the adoptee's history as they can whenever possible, which helps them to make sure the dog's new home will be a permanent one.

In most cases, the adoptee has been neutered so that there is no possibility of the dog further contributing to the very problem of overpopulation that put him in jeopardy to begin with. If the dog you select has not been sexually altered, the rescue groups can be very helpful in obtaining inexpensive or free neutering.

Miniature Poodle

Rhodesian Ridgebacks

Ibizan Hound

## Hounds

**Very small breeds (under 20 pounds):**

Dachshunds—Standard and Miniature

**Small- to Medium-Sized breeds (20 to 50 pounds):**

Basenji

Basset Hound

Beagle

Harrier

Norwegian Elkhound

Petit Basset Griffon Vendeen

Whippet

Large breeds (50 to 80 pounds):

Afghan Hound

Black and Tan Coonhound

American Foxhound

English Foxhound

Greyhound

Ibizan Hound

Pharaoh Hound

Rhodesian Ridgeback

Saluki

**Giant breeds (more than 80 pounds):**

Bloodhound

Borzoi

Irish Wolfhound

Otterhound

Scottish Deerhound

## Terriers

**Small- to medium-sized breeds (15 to 50 pounds):**

Australian Terrier

Bedlington Terrier

Border Terrier

Bull Terrier

Cairn Terrier

Dandie Dinmont Terrier

Smooth Fox Terrier

Wire Fox Terrier

Irish Terrier

Kerry Blue Terrier

Lakeland Terrier

Manchester Terrier (Standard)

Miniature Bull Terrier

Miniature Schnauzer

Norfolk Terrier

Norwich Terrier

Scottish Terrier

Sealyham Terrier

Skye Terrier

Soft Coated Wheaten Terrier

Staffordshire Bull Terrier

Welsh Terrier

West Highland White Terrier

**Large breeds (50 to 80 pounds):**

Airedale Terrier

American Staffordshire Terrier

Miniature Schnauzer

Airedale Terrier

Siberian Husky

Doberman Pinscher

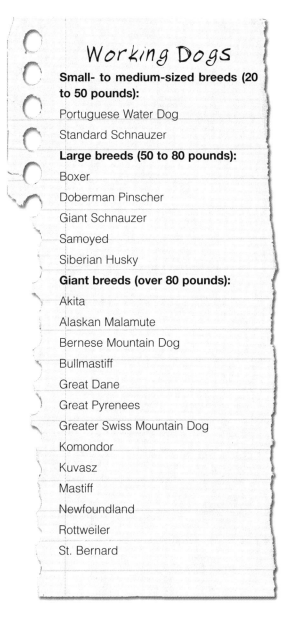

## Working Dogs

**Small- to medium-sized breeds (20 to 50 pounds):**

Portuguese Water Dog

Standard Schnauzer

**Large breeds (50 to 80 pounds):**

Boxer

Doberman Pinscher

Giant Schnauzer

Samoyed

Siberian Husky

**Giant breeds (over 80 pounds):**

Akita

Alaskan Malamute

Bernese Mountain Dog

Bullmastiff

Great Dane

Great Pyrenees

Greater Swiss Mountain Dog

Komondor

Kuvasz

Mastiff

Newfoundland

Rottweiler

St. Bernard

## TOYS

**All breeds in this group are small, ranging from 2 pounds to 20 pounds:**

Affenpinscher

Brussels Griffon

Chihuahua

Chinese Crested

English Toy Spaniel

Italian Greyhound

Japanese Chin

Maltese

Manchester Terrier—Toy

Miniature Pinscher

Papillon

Pekingese

Pomeranian

Poodle—Toy

Pug

Shih Tzu

Silky Terrier

Yorkshire Terrier

Miniature Pinscher

Italian Greyhound

French Bulldog

## Non-Sporting Dogs

**Very small breeds (under 15 pounds):**

Schipperke

Tibetan Spaniel

**Small- to medium-sized breeds (15 to 50 pounds):**

American Eskimo Dog

Bichon Frise

Boston Terrier

Bulldog

Shar Pei

Finnish Spitz

French Bulldog

Keeshond

Lhasa Apso

Poodle—Miniature

Shiba Inu

Tibetan Terrier

**Large breeds (50 to 80 pounds):**

Chow Chow

Dalmatian

Poodle—Standard

## Sporting Dogs

**Small- to medium-sized breeds (24 to 50 pounds):**

American Water Spaniel

Brittany

Cocker Spaniel

English Cocker Spaniel

English Springer Spaniel

Sussex Spaniel

Welsh Springer Spaniel

**Large breeds (50 to 80 pounds):**

Chesapeake Bay Retriever

Clumber Spaniel

Curly-Coated Retriever

English Setter

Flat-Coated Retriever

German Shorthaired Pointer

German Wirehaired Pointer

Golden Retriever

Gordon Setter

Irish Setter

Irish Water Spaniel

Labrador Retriever

Pointer

Vizsla

Weimaraner

Wirehaired Pointing Griffon

Brittany Spaniel

Weimaraner and Vizsla

Bouvier des Flandres

## Herding Dogs

**Small- to medium-sized breeds (15 to 50 pounds):**

Australian Cattle Dog

Bearded Collie

Border Collie

Cardigan Welsh Corgi

Pembroke Welsh Corgi

Puli

Shetland Sheepdog

**Large breeds (50 to 80 pounds):**

Australian Shepherd

Belgian Malinois

Belgian Sheepdog

Belgian Turvuren

Bouvier des Flandres

Briard

Collie—Rough and Smooth

German Shepherd

Old English Sheepdog

Pembroke Welsh Corgi

# Getting Ready

Planning ahead will help a great deal in making a puppy's or adult dog's transition from his familiar surroundings to the new and strange world you are providing for him. It can be disconcerting for a young pup when his mother and littermates suddenly disappear, and he is thrust into an entirely new environment where there is nothing but unfamiliar people and strange smells. Even adult dogs are somewhat bewildered by all the changes that seem to be taking place in their lives. An adopted adult dog has no idea of all the wonderful plans you may have in store for him; all he knows is that he is in a strange and somewhat frightening place.

Although it is not always possible, an ideal plan would be to visit your puppy or dog at his current

Shower your puppy with lots of love and attention.

A puppy raised in a happy environment will grow into a well-adjusted adult dog.

home so that you are not a complete stranger to him when you pick him up. If this is not practical, perhaps you will be able to take something from the dog's former home with you–like a blanket or toy of some kind or anything that will help the dog adjust to his new surroundings and survive the feeling of having nothing familiar in his life.

The best time to bring a new puppy or dog into your home is when you will be available to set aside a block of time to spend with him. A summer vacation is perfect, but only if you can plan on being home for the summer. Don't bring a new dog home and then pack him off to a boarding kennel while you take a three-week cruise.

If your vacation is not the right time, try to introduce your dog to his new home at the beginning of a long weekend, so you will have at least a couple of days to help the newcomer get over his homesickness blues.

Just as humans prepare for the arrival of a new baby by creating a checklist of things to do and equipment to buy, the new dog owner should be organizing his or her home for the puppy's arrival.

A sectioned-off area in the kitchen or bathroom is the ideal place to start your puppy off. Accidents can easily be cleaned up off the tile floors of these rooms. The kitchen is an especially suitable place because there is normally a good deal of traffic and noise, which helps to accustom the newcomer to day-to-day living in your household.

Don't forget that a young puppy is accustomed to the companionship of his littermates. Without them,

### Did You Know?

The worst time of the year to bring a puppy or dog into your home is during the Christmas holidays. If you are giving the puppy as a Christmas present, take a photograph of the pup or clip a picture of a similar-looking dog from a magazine and put it in a card under the tree. Include a note telling the recipient when (after Christmas) and where the pup can be collected. This also gives the person an opportunity to say "Thanks, but no thanks," if the idea was all yours and not suitable for them.

he will be lonely and it will be up to you to compensate for the absence of his siblings. At the same time, you must not let the puppy do whatever he chooses for the first few days and then suddenly expect him to start following rules that prohibit him from doing exactly those same things. Being permissive in this respect is not being kind, because it only confuses the puppy. Much of this applies to the adopted adult dog as well. Young puppies are not the only ones that may suffer from loneliness. All dogs entering a new living arrangement will need discipline, patience, and comfort.

## Where Will Your Dog Stay?

If you are like many people, your new puppy or dog will eventually end up sleeping in your bed. However, only permit this behavior when you are absolutely sure of the dog's ability to last the night without having to relieve himself, and you are sure that he will not spend the night getting into mischief of a costly nature. Prior to that time, I strongly suggest you designate a place where the puppy or dog can be secure and safe.

### Partitioned-Off Living Area

Paneled fence partitions in variable heights are available at most major pet shops and are well worth the investment, because they keep a puppy or small dog where you want him to be. Puppies and even grown dogs love to be where their owners are, but their being underfoot when you are busy can be hazardous to both dog and owner. The partitions create a safe area that will benefit both of you and can be used throughout your dog's lifetime.

*A puppy's littermates offer him a sense of security and safety.*

## Thinking Ahead

Well before the day your new dog or puppy is scheduled to arrive, you should be making notes on the things that need to get accomplished. Many of the items you will require can be obtained at any major pet emporium. It is a good idea to get to know the staff at your pet outlet. In most cases, these people have had extensive experience in the pet supply field and can offer invaluable advice on how to best care for your dog. They deal with dog owners day in and day out and may have excellent suggestions, even on where to obtain those items you will need that most pet shops aren't likely to carry.

**Part 1**

A fenced-in area gives your dog room to play while keeping him safe.

An outdoor playpen gives your puppy the freedom to exercise safely.

## Dutch Solution

We had a Boxer that absolutely hated being left in the kitchen alone—the place we had decided she would be least apt to get into trouble when we were gone. She objected to being on the other side of that closed door even when we were at home but in a different part of the house. A friend suggested a Dutch or half door might be an alternative. We had a carpenter build one for us and our problem was solved. Miss Busy didn't feel totally shut off from the rest of the house and never complained again. There are many ways to keep your dog safe, yet still allow him to feel involved in the household activities.

### Baby Gates

In the case of larger dogs, fence panels may be impractical. However, the kitchen is still an ideal place to keep a dog. A barrier or baby gate can be used to close off rooms and will restrict the puppy's access to the rest of the house.

### Playpens

People who live in a carpeted apartment or a home with elaborate and expensive wood flooring may not wish to have their dogs relieve themselves on the floor–even when papers are put down. Puppy playpens can be useful if you have a very small dog or tiny puppy and do not want to leave him on the floor.

Although children's playpens can be used, they can be hazardous in some cases. Those with wooden bars create the danger of a dog squeezing through or even catching his head between the bars, and the playpens that have plastic mesh sides can be chewed by an industrious youngster. If a puppy playpen seems like the appropriate enclosure for your dog, discuss the situation with your pet shop salesperson. There are all kinds of elevated playpens made

Part 1

especially for dogs. They are available in a wide array of sizes and are constructed of several different materials.

## Outdoor Runs and Fencing

It takes growing up and having children of their own before some people begin to realize just what their mother was really saying when she would suggest they go outside and play for awhile! There are times when life becomes so burdensome and hectic that we need space, literally and figuratively.

A large, enclosed area helps keep your puppy out of mischief.

A safe, secure outdoor run for your dog can be a true godsend. It allows you time to regroup and gives your best pooch some outdoor fun and exercise.

### Did You Know?

Fencing manufacturers are now producing portable panels of varying heights that are constructed as solidly as any in-ground fencing. These panels make it easy to frequently change the location of your dog run or to take it with you when you move.

I suggest a securely enclosed run even if your entire yard is fenced. When dogs are busy chasing squirrels or digging for a buried treasure, they are not thinking about your treasured tulip patch or Kentucky Blue Grass lawn that is the envy of the entire neighborhood. Also, most property fences average about five feet in height, which can be scaled without a second thought by the more acrobatic dog. Some dogs believe a barrier is just that and wouldn't think of trying to get over it; others are absolutely ingenious at figuring their way up, over, or under any fence that exists.

It's important that your dog understands his physical boundaries.

Although an exercise pen is useful, don't keep your dog enclosed for extended periods of time.

### Electrical Fences

Many areas throughout the country restrict the use of fencing, and some locations do not permit fences of any kind between properties. Thus electric fences have become very popular. No barrier is involved–the effectiveness of the system relies on an underground wire surrounding the property or the area in which the dog is confined. A battery-powered collar on the dog emits a shock when the wire is crossed.

There are some dogs that learn their boundaries very quickly and nothing known to dog or man would ever lure them past those limits. On the other hand, there are dogs–like some of the terriers or mixed breeds that may have inherited their high threshold of pain from some remote terrier ancestor–that have no reaction to the shocks emitted by the collars.

It should also be understood that the electrical fencing keeps your dog in but does nothing to keep other dogs out, because they aren't wearing the battery

### Climbing the Walls

When I was in the army, our company mascot was a Shetland Sheepdog (my idea!). Rebel joined us when she was eight weeks old and no bigger than a minute. The two-foot picket fence outside our headquarters was a more than adequate enclosure for her, and there was never any need to increase the height of the fence as she grew. The little area remained Rebel's territory from which she never strayed. She would rest her chin on one of the top bars of the fence and watch the world go by, but she never considered scaling the lilliputian barrier.

On the other hand, my first Boxer could have scaled the Berlin Wall without batting an eye! Ginger had no intention of staying behind—ever! The only place we felt truly confident in leaving her was safely inside the house.

## Part of the Family

Regardless of which fencing method you select or how secure the system is, the worst thing you could possibly do is push your dog out the door and expect him to spend day in and day out without human contact. This absolutely does not work for dogs! Throwing a pan of food down once or twice a day and changing his water is not sufficient socialization for any dog, regardless of breed. No dog should be forced to endure treatment of this kind. Those that are subjected to this neglect become destructive and neurotic, and in some cases, downright dangerous.

collar. Therefore, your female in heat is totally unprotected, and if a neighborhood dog roves around just waiting to pick a fight, your own dog is in open territory. Obviously, the effectiveness of these systems vary considerably from dog to dog and from one area to the next.

# **3**

# Welcome Home

A comfortable living environment equals a happy dog.

## Preparing for Your Puppy's Arrival

Once you have decided where your dog will initially spend most of his time, you have to think about making that place as comfortable and appealing to him as possible, whether the place you have chosen is a playpen or a corner of the kitchen.

Although you may plan on giving your dog access to the entire house at some point, do not do so at first. Even a dog that is entirely housetrained and completely accustomed to staying home alone in one place has to learn the lay of the land, so to speak, in his new residence. Where to go out, how to go out, what furniture is off limits–these are all things that even the best-trained house dog in the world has to

Your dog will consider his private space a quiet retreat.

### Did You Know?

Bean bag pillows come in sizes that will accommodate any dog from a Chihuahua to a Great Dane. They are light in weight, come covered in just about any kind of fabric or vinyl you might choose, and dogs love sleeping on them.

A word of caution—what looks good to you may also look good to your dog—good enough to eat! Before investing in a complete designer boudoir ensemble for your dog, be sure that it will not be devoured in an night of boredom.

learn. That first week is usually one filled with lots of "Okays" and "Nos!"

### Crates

Inside the fenced-off area, playpen, or room you have selected for your new dog, there should be a crate for him to sleep in. Buy a crate that will accommodate your dog's adult size. However, if this is too large for a tiny puppy, there are partitions available that adjust the space to fit the puppy's current size. The value of the use of the crate is discussed later in the book. Save yourself time, aggravation, and a lot of cleanup by adding this item to your list of necessities.

### Bedding

Once your dog is thoroughly housetrained and you decide that his crate is not elegant enough, the two of you can go shopping for a doggy bed that will accommodate your pal and satisfy your aesthetic bent. When you arrive at this point, you may decide that you want your dog to sleep in your bedroom but not on your bed. In that case, you can purchase a doggy bed made expressly for that purpose. I have seen some custom-designed beds that royalty, were they of a diminutive size, would have been delighted to sleep in.

### Water Dish and Feeding Bowl

These are available in many different materials. Choose something that is nonbreakable and not easy to tip over. A rambunctious puppy will very quickly learn to upset the water bowl and relish turning his entire living area into a swimming pool! Stainless steel bowls are recommended because they eliminate the worry of the toxic content in some plastics, and dogs and puppies are not beyond chewing (and trying to digest!) plastic bowls.

## Food

Diet and feeding schedules are discussed at great length later in the book. You probably will want to review that information before you go shopping, especially if feeding instructions were not given to you when you purchased your new dog. If you still do not feel confident that you will make the right choice of food, your veterinarian or the staff at your pet supply store are always helpful in this respect. Remember, however, that abruptly switching food could create a bowel upset for the dog and a huge mess for you.

Regardless of what brand of food or feeding plan you will be putting your dog on in the future, bring home a couple of days worth of the food your dog has been accustomed to eating. You can gradually change his diet to whatever you feel is best for him, if that change is necessary.

*Sturdy food dishes will help prevent messy accidents.*

## Brushes and Combs

Again, your pet shop can help you pick out the type of grooming equipment you will need. There are different combs and brushes for all coat types and lengths. Take your dog along with you, if possible, because it will assist your making the proper selection.

## Collar and Leash

Just as there are many brands of food, there are also varieties of different leashes, collars, and harnesses to choose from. There is probably a collar and leash for practically everything you will ever want your dog to learn or do for the rest of both of your lives.

First things first—for puppy training and leash breaking, there are soft fabric collars available that weigh next to nothing. For the adult dog, initially I suggest two

*Grooming should be a part of your puppy's daily routine.*

This puppy gets used to his new collar.

### The Right Stuff

Lightweight plastic or fabric leashes are good for the young puppy, but you will eventually want to invest in an appropriately strong leather or flexi-lead. You can use a piece of string to measure the circumference of your dog's neck. Take this along with you to the pet shop where you purchase your initial supplies, and the salesperson will be able to assist you in obtaining the correct size collar. Better yet, most pet supply establishments are dog-friendly and allow—actually invite—your dog to come shopping with you.

collars: A buckle collar for everyday use to which you will attach your dogs rabies tag, license, and identification, and a second collar to be used only during training sessions. There are a number of choices for the latter, but my training collar recommendations are covered later in the training section of the book.

### Training Equipment

The proper collars and leashes will definitely assist you in getting the training message across to your dog and will eliminate the need for feeling like the villain when it comes to corrections. For instance, just the sound of a link-chain collar when it is jerked will let your dog know he is doing something wrong. When you decide how far you want to take your training, you can invest in the proper equipment.

### Toys

Do dogs need toys? Yes! Do they need one of every toy that is offered for sale? An emphatic no! Puppies and new dogs do need several toys of different kinds to keep them occupied, exercised, and out of mischief. However, don't give your dog so many toys that the dog begins to think everything that exists is a toy to chew on.

A variety of safe toys like NYlabones® can help keep your dog occupied.

The toys you do choose can be anything that is appropriate for the size and the age of the dog–just be sure the toys are safe and do not have buttons or strings that can be chewed off or swallowed. Also, avoid balls made of soft material that can be chewed apart and hard plastic toys that can splinter easily.

Make sure any toys you give a puppy or even grown dog are too large to become lodged in the mouth or caught in the throat. Bones can be instrumental in keeping your dog's jaw and teeth occupied and your belongings safe, especially with teething puppies. Large knuckle bones may not seem like toys, but your dog will undoubtedly think otherwise. A dog can spend the best part of an afternoon gnawing away on the same bone!

*This puppy is trying out his new teeth on a NYlabone®.*

A Rhino™ toy is wonderful because it is made of nearly indestructible rubber. It has a hole in the bottom so that a little dab of peanut butter or some other treat can be stuffed into it. This toy will keep dogs occupied for hours on end.

### No Shoes

Never give your puppy old or discarded shoes to play with. A puppy is unable to determine the difference between old and new. As far as he is concerned, an old slipper smells and tastes exactly like a pair of high heels you may have only worn a time or two.

Teddy bears or stuffed animals that are not made specifically for dogs are not a good idea. Most of them have plastic or glass buttons for eyes that can be swallowed. Even with those removed, they are risky. Ears can be torn off and swallowed or the stuffing ripped out and ingested. Some dogs treat stuffed animals with great love and affection for weeks and months, and then suddenly, as punishment for some offense of which we have no knowledge, a dog decides to totally dismantle and swallow Mr. Teddy's innards. You and your dog may have to spend some very unpleasant and costly time at the veterinarian's office when this happens.

## Bringing Your Puppy Home

The safest way to transport a puppy from the kennel to your home is to obtain a pet carrier or cardboard box large enough for the puppy to comfortably stretch out in. Make sure the sides are high enough so that the puppy cannot climb out. Put a layer of newspapers at the bottom in case of accidents and a soft blanket or towel on top of that.

An adult dog may or may not be accustomed to riding in a car. A dog that hasn't been conditioned to doing so can be become extremely carsick. Because you wont know this until you're riding along, I strongly suggest having someone do the driving while you sit in the back seat with your dog to deal with any mess that may occur. If you can't find a volunteer to drive, cover your back seat with a blanket or heavy toweling and place the dog there.

## Pups and Children

You must take precautions to ensure the safety of both your dog and your children when they first meet. This holds true until such a time when both child and dog can be fully trusted to handle each other with care. In some cases, the dog/child relationship takes time to develop, and until it has reached a point where tolerance and respect between the two has been well established, adults should always be on hand to supervise.

Once a good relationship has been established, it is amazing how well children and dogs are able to communicate and bond with each other. In some primal way, without the use of words, they can express countless emotions, including devotion and trust in each other, that very few adults are privileged to enjoy.

Many parents believe that having a dog in their child's life teaches responsibility. Certainly this is true, as long as the parent is there to teach the child just how dependent a dog really is on his owner. The parent must also be on hand to take control of situations that a child is incapable of handling.

This child and puppy share a mutual admiration.

Chores that include taking care of the dog's daily needs teach the child that there are things that we do that are not necessarily just for fun. Of course, this does encourages responsibility, but it also teaches a subtle lesson as well. Children begin to recognize the fact that creatures

## Safe Play

Children should never be allowed to chase a puppy or new dog, and there should always be a place of refuge for the dog to retreat to when necessary. Your children should never encourage a puppy's playful puppy bites or allow the puppy to chase them around the house in fun. Growling, biting, and chasing may appear cute and are harmless in the young dog, but they are habits that can become extremely difficult to correct as the puppy

other than themselves also have needs, and this assists them in realizing that things exist outside of their own little world.

Children are also able to learn that there are some things that are absolutely forbidden in their relationship with their dog, even though they may seem like great fun. Many wise old dogs will let a toddler do almost anything to them without complaint. This is where the parent must step in, not only for the dog's safety but to teach the child right from wrong. Gentleness and consideration are prerequisites when caring for animals, and the value of these qualities in human relationships is certainly not to be underestimated.

### The New Arrival

Your new dog has settled in, has begun to follow the daily routine, and seldom breaks any of the household rules. All seems to be going well, until suddenly what once was just the three of you now becomes a quartet. There's a new baby in the house!

It is impossible to make a blanket judgment about how all dogs will react to an infant. One thing that is certain, however, is that the dog that you can rely on to handle the situation well is the dog that is well trained. A dog that can only be relied upon to obey some of the time cannot be trusted to keep his curiosity in check when it comes to a new baby.

A dog should never be allowed to approach an infant unattended by an adult, and the dog should know he can only proceed to investigate at the speed dictated by his owner. All those basic training lessons need to be reinforced. You must now know for certain that you and your dog are perfectly clear on the meaning of the words no, sit, stay, and come.

Prepare your dog for the new arrival by letting him

*It's important for children to understand responsible pet ownership.*

## Dogs and Babies

If you are expecting a new infant in the home, there are a number of important questions that must be answered.

1. Has your dog been exposed to children in the past? As I have mentioned before, first encounters with these miniature people are quite startling for some dogs.

2. Has your dog had any experience with infants? Infants can cry, kick, and scream, which excites some dogs and awakens a predatory instinct in others.

3. As amiable as they might be toward adults, some dogs, for reasons known only to them, do not like children. Does this describe your dog?

4. Does your dog aggressively try to protect you from other dogs and people? A dog with this kind of temperament may consider a child a threat and act aggressively toward the child, or may consider the child part of his turf and act aggressively toward anyone who comes near the child.

get accustomed to the baby's room and scent. Familiarize him with the layout and smell of the baby's room, and if possible, give him something that the baby has worn before he or she arrives.

The lifelong bond between a child and puppy can be very special.

Introductions should be gradual and conducted only when you and the dog are calm and there is not a great deal of confusion. In fact, it is best to allow the dog to check out the infant when just you and only one other person are present. Another person is needed primarily to have the dog on leash and to hold on to the leash while you are holding the baby, making the necessary introductions. Attempting this on your own can become difficult if the dog has an adverse reaction to the child.

As children mature, they can begin to appreciate the companionship that a dog provides. There are many

## Did You Know?

Never leave an infant on the floor unless you are there to supervise. The friendliest dog with the best of intentions may decide he wants to play and begin prodding the infant with his front feet. Even the tiniest dog can injure an infant by accidentally stepping on the baby or scratching the child's skin with his nails. Never leave your child and your dog alone when unsupervised until the child is old enough to be trusted to handle himself and the dog.

different activities that a child can participate in with their dog. By working, living, and playing together, the child and his canine pal can form a loving and trusting relationship.

## Car Travel

Part of a dog's or puppy's socialization process will take place away from home. The puppy must learn to accept unfamiliar people and places, and the only way for the puppy to learn to take these changes in stride is to visit as many new sites and meet as many strangers as you can arrange.

### Did You Know?

Dogs that are first-time riders or those that are subject to becoming carsick should not be fed or watered for at least two to three hours before they take a trip. A full stomach can worsen an already difficult situation for these delicate canines.

Trips to the shopping mall or walks through the park will expose your young dog to new and different situations each time you are out. Of course, this should never be attempted until your puppy has had all of his inoculations. Once that is completed, you are both ready to set off to meet the world, and this often involves riding in a car.

When the puppy seems to accept short rides happily, the length of time in the car can be increased gradually until you see that the puppy is truly enjoying the outings. Even those dogs and puppies suffering from the most severe cases of carsickness seem to respond to this approach and soon begin to consider the car a second home. If your dog's carsickness continues, speak to your veterinarian. He or she can prescribe medication that can help to alleviate the problem.

The safest way to transport your dog is in a carrier, with the door securely latched. Many station wagons accommodate partitions commonly referred to as dog guards. These safety devices confine dogs to the rear portion of the car. These simple safety precautions might one day save the life of your pet.

Take precautions to ensure your dog's safety when riding in the car.

It's a good idea to attach identification tags to your puppy's collar.

## Open Windows

It is important to make it a practice to never leave your dog alone in the car with the windows closed. Even on cool days, the sun beating down on a closed car can send the inside temperature soaring. Leaving a dog alone in an unventilated car could easily cause his death.

Even when conditions permit the windows to be left open, it is still dangerous, because open windows risk your dog's escape and invite theft. Thieves are not beyond stealing dogs! An unrestrained dog in a car with open windows courts disaster.

### Tags

Any time your dog leaves your home, he should be wearing a collar with identification tags attached. Many times, dogs are thrown clear of the car in an accident but become so frightened that they run blindly away. Not knowing where they are and not carrying any means of identification, a dog may be lost forever.

## Car Safety

Some words of caution about dogs and cars: As much as it might seem more enjoyable to have your puppy or adult dog ride unrestrained in the car or on the seat beside you, it can be extremely dangerous. An overly enthusiastic canine passenger can interfere with the driver's control or divert the driver's attention. Also, a sudden stop can hurl your dog against the front window, severely injuring or even killing him.

### Home Is Where the Heart Is

Once home, the first order of business is to get the new member of your clan to the little corner of your house he will call his home for a while. You may be tempted to invite the whole gang in to view the new arrival, and if you have children, they will undoubtedly have everyone in the neighborhood standing at the door. Resist temptation and hold the throngs back for a couple of days. Your new friend will be doing just about all he can to handle the changes that have already transpired. Don't add more confusion to the issue.

Get the new dog accustomed to the sights, sounds, and smells of his new surroundings. There are all kinds of in-house introductions that will have to be made. Save the neighborhood for later.

### Did You Know?

A puppy's first night or two in a new home will be strange and lonely for him. The pup will undoubtedly whine in search of his littermates, especially at night when there is no one to snuggle up to. For the first few nights after the new puppy arrives, put his crate next to your bed and let the newcomer sleep there. If the puppy wakes up crying from loneliness, a reassuring hand can be dropped down into the box, and you won't have to trudge to a different part of the house to quiet the lonely puppy.

Strange noises, children, and other animals can be bewildering for the dog that is not accustomed to them. Gradually introduce your dog to such sounds as the stereo, the television set, and the garbage disposal. Hopefully, the first time your puppy or even adult dog is exposed to any strange, loud sounds, you will be able to keep the sound limited to just a second or two. Once it appears there is no eminent threat of danger, you will be able to increase the length of time and the volume.

## Other Pets

Your new dog's introduction to other animals in the household must be carefully supervised. A puppy will love the world and all the creatures in it—even at a very early age, puppies are incredibly inquisitive. This characteristic can get a puppy into trouble with senior animals in the household.

The family cat that is not accustomed to dogs and dogs that have not been raised around cats may have a lot of adjusting to do. Some cats hold their ground until the intruder gets close enough to receive a good smack across the snout. Smart cat! Sometimes this is all it takes to put even the biggest, boldest dog in a one-down position. Some cats may react violently to the unwelcomed advances of a bold puppy. Know your cat and allow the first meeting to take place gradually, through an enclosure, if at all possible.

Little rodents or birds may represent toys, even to dogs with the most amiable of temperaments, and that toy just might wind up in the dog's mouth. Save introductions of this kind until you get some sense of how your puppy or grown dog might approach the little critters.

Puppies need to be introduced to new people and places gradually.

*Sniffing is a dog's way of saying "hello."*

For all these reasons, it is very important to confine the newcomer so that the other pets in the household are not constantly harassed before they have had time to fully accept the puppy or grown dog. The partitioned area set up to accommodate the new puppy that was described earlier will give the senior members of the household's animal kingdom an opportunity to inspect the new arrival at their leisure without having to endure unsolicited attention.

Adult dogs may be accustomed to challenging strange dogs or chasing cats. Once properly introduced and supervised, the new dog and the upperclassmen may or may not decide to become bosom buddies. Many dog owners tell of their dogs getting along famously with resident dogs, cats, and even other small animals—some to the point of appointing themselves guardians and protectors.

## Dog-Proofing Your Home

A good part of keeping your new dog safe depends upon your ability to properly dog-proof your home. Electrical outlets, lamp cords, strings, and mouth-sized objects of any kind all spell danger to the inquisitive newcomer. If you think of your new arrival as both super sleuth

### Two or More Dogs

Whether the dogs concerned are neutered or not, your best bet in bringing a second dog into your family is to choose one of the opposite sex. Although most sexually altered males get along with each other just fine, there are always exceptions, and with some dogs, this could lead to a very testy situation.

Bringing a second adult male dog into your home can be tricky, especially in some of the more aggressive breeds. Two entire male dogs (i.e., dogs that have not been neutered) in the same household will always bear watching. Problems between two females are usually less likely, but not entirely unheard of. Introductions should always be handled with care and consideration, with benefit of the doubt given to the resident. An adult dog with seniority may mistake a new puppy's exuberance for aggression and react accordingly.

> ## Did You Know?
> There are many common household and outdoor plants that could be life threatening to your dog. Keep the following well out of your dog's reach: azaleas, bird of paradise, calla lilies, dieffenbachia (dumb cane), elephants ear, hydrangea, larkspur, lily of the valley, mushrooms, philodendron, poinsettia, and tobacco.

*Most pets enjoy having other canine companions.*

and demolition expert, you will be better equipped to protect both your home and your dog.

Puppies, particularly, are experts at getting into places they shouldn't be. The important thing to remember is that neither an adult dog nor puppy will be able to chew a hole in your rug or pull the tablecloth and all its contents down on top of himself if he can't get to these off-limits items in the first place.

Things like household cleaning products, gardening supplies, and poisonous plants must be kept in securely latched cupboards or well out of the dog's reach. In the case of puppies, realize that they grow like weeds, and what a puppy can't reach today may be very reachable tomorrow.

There are many house plants that can make your puppy ill or even cause death. Most veterinarians will be able to supply you with a complete list of plants that are poisonous to dogs or capable of causing extreme reactions.

*Playtime should be fun and safe.*

There are baby gates to keep your puppy out, and cages, kennels, and paneled fence partitions of

Chewing is a natural part of a puppy's development.

Hugs and kisses are the key ingredients for puppy love.

various kinds to keep your puppy in. All this and a daily proofing patrol will help you and your pet avoid serious damage and potential danger.

### Chewing

Although it might appear otherwise, dogs do not chew out of spite. They can be terribly destructive, and there may come at a time when you feel quite certain they are getting back at you for something, but this is definitely not the case. What appears to be a case of getting even is far more apt to be the result of anxiety caused by being punished after the fact and having no idea why. Dogs chew out of boredom, to relieve anxiety, and simply because it feels and tastes good.

However, all those rational reasons do not put the leg back on your new table or the cover on your first edition. Some dogs chew more than others, and puppies chew most of all (it relieves pressure on those gums through which new teeth are pushing). It may sound terribly elementary, but keeping things that you don't want chewed out of the dog's reach goes a long way toward circumventing this nasty habit.

Of course, it isn't possible to stow the living room sofa or the hallway oriental rug away every time your dog appears on the scene. Those are situations in which you must have your pal secured in a crate or playpen you keep on hand. Also, there is a product that is a bitter tasting spray. It is actually a furniture cream that is nonpoisonous and can be used to coat electrical wires and chair legs. Usually, dogs hate its taste and will avoid any object to which the product has been applied. Do note that I say "usually" because there is always the occasional dog that is not deterred by the unpleasant taste in the least. For the average dog that the product does discourage, the cream can be used not only to protect household items, but many breeders use the product on the dogs to prevent them from chewing on themselves.

For the dog that is not deterred from chewing by this product, there is plastic tubing available at hardware stores that can be put around electrical cords and furniture legs. I wouldn't rely too heavily on the plastic tubing, however, because most dogs are quicker at chewing through it than most of us are capable of putting it down. The message here is never to underestimate your puppy's ability to get into mischief. Even adult dogs have those occasional lapses into puppyhood. Securing the dog when you aren't there to supervise what's going on will save you a lot of replacement shopping.

*Dogs are known to follow their noses anywhere.*

### Strangers in the House

Many households experience more traffic flow during the holidays than they do at any other time of the year. Guests who are unaccustomed to living with dogs do not realize that leaving doors ajar can lead to disaster. Holiday visitors who do not own dogs do not stop to think a little turkey bone could cause choking or that food that the family dog is unaccustomed to eating could cause acute diarrhea.

It is important to realize that Mom is usually called upon to add significantly to her normal duties during the holidays, so watching the puppy and keeping an eye on the guests should definitely be a family affair. It is also worth remembering that not everyone entering the household will adore your little rascal as much as you do. Some dogs are not terribly discerning about who they give a big wet kiss to or on whose

### Holiday Precautions

Without a doubt, the holidays can provide more possibilities for your dog to find his way into trouble than at any other time of the year. All the precautions that must be taken during the normal course of the year still apply, but those special days (or weeks) of the year require even more diligence.

## Deck the Halls

Those shiny decorations, paper ornaments, and balloons can continue to deck the halls, but make sure they do so well above puppy level. As far as dogs are concerned, shiny trinkets, strings, and rubber balloons belong in the mouth. New plants, flowers, and berries also look very appetizing to a dog that has not experienced many holidays and, as we have said before, the plants could very easily be poisonous. Just remember—what goes into a dog's mouth will invariably wind up in his stomach—digestible or not.

A puppy should always be handled with care.

new black suit they deposit their hair. Be considerate of your guests and of your dog by making sure guests want your fluffy bundle of hair's attention and by putting him safely out of the way in his crate during party times.

### Treat Dangers

The holidays are a great excuse for people to indulge in gourmet treats if they so choose. Food that dogs are unaccustomed to can create upset stomachs, and diarrhea is almost invariably a result. Few households need a dog with diarrhea, acute or otherwise, during hectic holiday affairs.

Holidays are also the time of year during which chocolate lovers have a field day. Chocolates on low tables are an invitation to disaster for a puppy or mature dog. Children are not past poking their fingers into chocolates to find out what is inside (I wasn't!). If the tested piece happens to be something the child might not care for, there is no telling where the discarded candy might go. Chocolate contains a natural caffeine called theobromine that has been known to kill some dogs. Do not allow your dog to have chocolate and caution everyone in the family against this danger.

# Fitting In—The Family Unit

## Choosing the Right Dog for You

There should be no doubt at this point how important compatibility is when you are attempting to make your dog part of the family unit. If a dog has already taken up residence in your household, your job is to make the relationship work. If you haven't yet selected your dog, there is a good deal you can to do in advance to make sure your selection is one that will work out well.

Just as there are personality differences within children of the same family, so are there temperament differences among puppies coming from the same litter, and this holds true whether the litter is purebred or of mixed ancestry. Although we aren't going to find enormous contrasts in

Choose the puppy that best fits your personality.

**Chapter 4**

Labs are playful, energetic, and fun-loving.

A puppy's interactions with his littermates tell a lot about his temperament.

instinctive behavior within a litter (i.e., a Bulldog becoming a herding dog), there most certainly will be differences in how each puppy approaches life. Being aware of these differences will tell you a great deal about how suitable a puppy will be for your family.

A rock-n-roll type of family environment in which there is constant loud music playing, doors slamming, seemingly endless parties, and a steady flow of strangers coming and going will to be a very difficult place for the passive, retiring puppy to adjust. On the other hand, the quiet family, whose members are soft spoken and inclined toward quiet evenings together reading or perhaps watching television are going to find life with a furry tornado difficult, if not impossible. This family will find little joy in the dog that never stops to rest and reacts to every sound–even those yet to be made–vocally.

If the household already includes other pets, bringing home an extremely domineering adult dog or one that is extremely aggressive is obviously going to upset the social balance that has already been established. Therefore, it is wise to be aware of the differences that exist within puppies of the same litter and in adult dogs so that their integration into the family unit can work smoothly and provide enjoyment rather than trauma.

## Temperaments

If your new puppy or adult dog is being obtained from an experienced and respected breeder, you can rest assured that he or she will know a great deal about the dog's personality. This will help considerably in making your choice. Temperaments tests given to puppies and dogs that are adopted from animal shelters and rescue organizations can be of help in determining whether or not your choice is a good one. Puppies are the easiest to figure out. Simply observing them with their littermates can tell you a great deal about their personalities.

## Leader of the Pack

Whether purebred or mixed breed, there's always the pup in the litter that has declared himself the leader of the pack. You won't miss this one. Pack leaders are first at everything (even if they don't get there first!). They'll bully their way through to the top spot or wind up with the best toy nine times out of ten. Some behaviorists also believe that the leader types have the fastest heartbeats of any of the puppies in a litter–up to 2 percent faster, in many cases. Naturally, you aren't expected to arrive at the home of your puppy-to-be with stethoscope in hand, but in handling the puppies in the litter, you may well detect the difference in their heartbeats.

*These puppies play follow the leader.*

Leader-type puppies need leader-type owners. This kind of puppy will undoubtedly grow up loving you as much as any of his littermates, but do not expect this dog to be panting to please you at every turn.

Unfortunately, the person who likes a dominant kind of pup finds great amusement in the pup's aggressive behavior–growling, mouthing, biting, and generally indicating what a little toughie he is. Perhaps this is cute in puppyhood, but encouraging that behavior enforces these aggressive tendencies, and it can be next to impossible to change the dog's mind in adulthood.

### The Right Owner

One reason (and a very bad reason I might add) that some people are attracted to big dogs stems from what I call macho-mentality. Perhaps to make up for something else, they want the biggest, toughest dog on the block. Someone who has this mentality will be attracted to the pack-leader puppy, but when and if they do select this puppy, it is critical that the person have the ability and facilities to properly care for this kind of dog.

The dominant, leader-type dog cannot be allowed to make choices on his own. This is particularly true of large dogs. The combination of size and aggressiveness can be dangerous, and the negligent owner will undoubtedly have to pay the consequences at some point.

### The Adventurer

The adventure lover in the litter puts up with the leader and stands his own ground if he has to. He would, however, rather quietly investigate what is going on in his world. This kind of personality could be a good choice for a busy family, because he won't need as much babysitting and won't be thrown by all the hustle and bustle of children.

This pup is more eager to please you than the litter's pack leader, but that doesn't mean he is a total pushover. He could be inclined to be a bit independent simply because he likes to go his own way. The adventurer is usually inclined to be somewhat gregarious and capable of sharing his affection with all members of the family.

You might think this puppy is boring because he may not stand out from his littermates—neither terribly aggressive nor shy. But given his own family to live with, the adventurer could be one of those wonderful dogs that is a joy to own and that presents relatively few problem behaviors.

The ideal pet can accept other animals and people easily.

### The Passive Pup

Don't confuse the passive type of puppy with one that is downright shy. He is apt to allow his littermates to take what they want and will avoid serious tussles at all costs. While the passive pup doesn't run and cower, he would probably be more than happy to walk the proverbial mile to avoid a confrontation. This youngster does best with a steady, supportive owner who offers lots of attention and patience.

The passive dog needs constant reassurance and could easily develop the nudging technique to remind you that he thinks being petted and praised around the clock would be just fine. You may also have to work a bit to assure him that your walking out the door is not the end of the world.

In the right hands, the more passive pet could be a whiz at learning because his goal in life is usually to please. Compliance won't be a problem, but you must be careful that you aren't too aggressive or heavy-handed in your training techniques.

## The Shy Pup

This is truly a problem child, but his problems are at the opposite end of the spectrum from his pack-leader littermate. This puppy seems to react in fear to almost everything–littermates that play too rough, loud noises, strange people, etc. People who are not aware of what the situation really is are apt to assume that the puppy has been abused, when that is not the case at all.

I can remember one occasion in particular in which I had a shy puppy born to a litter in which all the other puppies had absolutely delightful temperaments. He evidenced this behavior right from the time his eyes first opened and he began walking around the whelping box. His treatment and experiences were no different than those of the other puppies. Try as I might, I was never really able to conquer the puppy's unfounded fears.

Fortunately, I was able to come across kind and sympathetic owners for the pup. They were mature people with no children who understood the temperament difficulties and yet were happy to provide a home for him. The puppy was placed with the family under the provision that, in the event a problem arose that the new owner was not able to cope with, the puppy would be returned to us. In this particular case, however, the puppy grew to adulthood as a quiet, devoted pet. While he did improve in his shyness, new situations, strange people, or sudden loud noises were a problem throughout his entire life.

A good breeder will match the right puppy to the right home.

Give your puppy time to adjust to his new surroundings.

## The Suspicious Pup

I would be very concerned about anyone considering a puppy that was suspicious of strangers or one that was openly aggressive toward littermates or people. This kind of personality is totally uncharacteristic of a young puppy and could lead to dangerous behavior. If you suspect this temperament in a puppy, look elsewhere. Even in the guardian breeds, protective and territorial instincts develop with maturity—they are not characteristic of a young puppy.

Adopting an adult dog from a rescue or shelter can be very rewarding.

## Adult Temperaments

It won't take you a great deal of testing to tell if a grown dog is of a dominant or aggressive nature, nor will you be easily deceived by the shy dog. Each is very set in his ways, and each action and reaction can be potentially dangerous, particularly if there are children present in the new household.

A dog that challenges you in any way, that shows excessive fear, or that tries to run and escape should be left for the experienced trainer. Dogs of this nature require special care and handling that the average person is usually not capable of providing.

Dogs that are extremely excitable and whose exuberance cannot be quelled have no concept of how rough they are. They would certainly not be a wise choice for a home where there is toddler or an elderly person. Tractability is very important in a dog where care and consideration must be given to very young children, physically challenged people, or the elderly.

Spend time with an adult dog before you decide to take him home. Ask the volunteers at the shelter or rescue to give you all the information they have about his background, training, and health. Monitor his reaction to you as you approach him and play with him. Try to roll him over on to his back to see if he will accept a submissive position and give him a tummy rub. Look him in the eye and offer him a treat if possible. Introduce him to all family members, including children, and watch his reaction carefully. If the dog seems to pass all these tests without showing fear or aggression, take him home on a trial basis. An adopted adult dog can make a grateful and loyal

## Puppy Temperaments

There are a few techniques that can tell you a great deal about an individual puppy as well. Cradling a puppy in your arms and holding him on his back can tell you how willing the youngster is to comply with what you want him to do. Checking ears and feet can bring a number of different reactions. Some pups will easily comply; others will offer mild resistance. The puppy to avoid is the one that becomes terrified at the occurrence of something strange or the one that snaps at being intruded upon. No puppy should be anything less than happy, friendly, and reasonably able to cope with your little experiments.

There are more formal tests that behaviorists can give puppies that can reveal significant details in regard to their potential temperament as adults. These tests begin as early as three weeks and continue on up to three months.

## Body Language

When we meet people for the first time, we know nothing about them. Some of us are inclined to make judgments based on what the person says or on what others have said about the person. There are others of us who look and listen for clues that lie beyond what the speaker is saying, which can tell us far more about what we want to know than the spoken word. Because dogs do not have the ability to communicate with us through words, body language can play a big part in helping us to understand canine behavior.

Basic touch tests are a great way to gauge your puppy's temperament.

Understanding your dog's body language can help you to communicate with him.

This Rhodesian's body language shows that he is relaxed and friendly.

Dogs in the wild have communicated with each other through the use of barks, growls, and whines since they were all still wolves running the primordial forests. However, the major form of communication among wolves and dogs is through body language. Interestingly, the more familiar we become with canine body language, the more impressed we become with its simplicity and clarity. There are two basic attitudes present in canine body language that are keys to understanding the whole language: active and passive.

In a nutshell, active or dominant behavior is forward and upward, while passive behavior is backward and down. If your dog is about to challenge another dog, he will stand stiff legged, usually with the hair on the back of his neck and shoulders standing up. The dog's head will be up and he will look directly forward. The body will be taut and the tail carried stiff and erect. Often the teeth are bared and the aggressor will make a snarling noise. If the dog being challenged is equally aggressive, he will move forward with the same attitude and stance. Depending upon the degree of aggressiveness on the part of the two dogs, a fight may or may not ensue. If a dog displays this type of body language, he should be avoided.

If challenged, the passive or submissive dog reacts in an entirely opposite manner. He moves back and down, his head is lowered, his ears are pinned back, and his tail is tucked under his body. The teeth may be bared in sort of an embarrassed grid, but if any sound is made, it would most likely be a whimper. To show his submissiveness, he may roll over onto his back.

All dogs have the potential to display both submissive and dominant behavior. Only through experience and training do they learn the appropriate behavior for certain situations. Although canine body language goes far beyond these two stances, understanding the basics can tell us a great deal about what kind of behavior we can expect from our own dog. With this knowledge alone, we are better able to deal with our dogs in a more productive manner.

All dogs are different, and they react differently to similar situations. While no dog should be permitted to behave as he sees fit, your approach to his socialization will work best if you have a clear picture of the dog's temperament, personality, and approach toward life.

## Socialization

If there is one lesson that all dogs must learn, it is to get along well with people. That doesn't mean every dog must lavish affection on every person he meets. However, a dog must understand that humans lay down the rules and regulations in our society and that he must learn to abide by those rules without hesitation.

*Setting guidelines for your puppy will help him grow into a well-mannered adult.*

Sound temperament enables a dog to do this. Temperament is both inherited and learned. Poor treatment and lack of socialization can ruin inherited good temperament. A dog that has inherited a bad temperament is a nuisance at best and downright dangerous at worst. He will need professional assistance in order to become a good canine citizen and a trusted family member.

Socialization is a process that begins when a puppy is born and must continue when the dog arrives at your home. In fact, socialization must continue throughout the rest of your

### Did You Know?

A dog with a sound temperament can be introduced to the unending complications and stresses of modern living and survive them all. Children are particularly good at assisting their dogs to learn household rules and to cope with what has become our very modern and complex lifestyle. Puppies born or raised in homes with supervised children seem particularly good at adapting themselves to new environments. Children's giggles and laughter help developing puppies to become accustomed to different tones and inflections of voice. Because of their size, children seem less overwhelming to puppies. Perhaps these are just some of the reasons why puppies and children seem to develop such an affinity for each other.

*It's important that puppies learn how to get along with each other.*

dog's life with you. It is important to realize that a dog may be very happy and well behaved at home with you and your family, but if socialization is not continued, that sunny disposition will not extend outside your front door. From the day he arrives at your home, you must be committed to helping him meet and coexist with all human beings and animals. Don't worry about the dog's protective instinct. Protectiveness comes with maturity. Never encourage aggressive behavior on the part of a puppy. It is more important for your dog to be able to become a good canine citizen and accept all he meets.

Once you leave the confines of your home, everything you do will be an adventure for your new puppy or adult dog. Strangers will be met on the street, and it is up to you to teach your dog to meet them with a friendly attitude, as well as with restraint.

There is nothing more irritating than to go through all of the effort of responsibly training your dog only to have him harassed by an out-of-control and off-leash bully. If you and your dog are approached by an off-leash dog,

*The proper socialization is vital to your dog's well-being.*

### Cats and Dogs

Other dogs and cats exist, and you and your dog will have to get used to it. You may never be able to teach your dog to love other four-footed creatures, but he must understand that all those other animals have just as much right to the streets and parks as he does.

do not stop to let the two get acquainted! You do not know what the other dog's intentions are, and you could easily end up in the middle of a dog fight. Continue walking without acknowledging the presence of the intruder and do your best to keep your dog from doing so. Usually, off-leash dogs are most aggressive when they are defending their own turf. If it is you and your dog that are on the stranger's turf, the best advice is to exit the area as quickly as you can.

Obedience training can help improve your dog's behavior.

Even people who love dogs aren't particularly pleased to have a strange dog come galloping headlong down the street and fling himself at them. Granted, the dog may be exhibiting his joy and love for the world, but the stranger receiving the greeting doesn't know that. Teach your dog to practice his good manners when meeting others. Carry treats with you when you go out. Practice the sit command by making your dog sit and wait to get petted when he meets someone. If your puppy backs off from a stranger, give the person one of the doggie snacks and have him or her offer it to your puppy. Insist your young dog be amenable to the attention of any strangers of which you approve, regardless of sex, age, or race. Even dogs that are trained for personal protection are taught to stand and be touched by a stranger if their owner gives the command. It is not up to your puppy to decide whom he will or will not tolerate. You are in charge. You must call the shots.

Once your dog learns to accept people outside of his family, he can begin to form friendships and establish trust. This will make everyday life with your dog a pleasant experience.

**Did You Know?**

To assist socialization, your dog should go everywhere with you— the post office, park, beach, and shopping mall—wherever. This applies to puppies as well, once inoculations are current. The more people your dog meets, the better socialized he will become.

# Part Two
# Training Your Dog

"Betsy! Get off the phone! Once you start yapping, pretty soon the whole neighborhood is at it.""

# 5

# Housetraining and Puppy Training

Although a dog's temperament and personality can be determined by testing him before bringing him home, it certainly isn't necessary for every new dog owner to resort to extensive, professional testing. A good part of temperament is observable. However, I would seriously consider the input of a professional if I were adopting a mature dog of a larger size, particularly if there are children in the home and nothing is known of the dog's history. It is important to understand that not all dogs have the same personality. Even puppies from the same litter and same breed can have vastly different approaches to life. A perfect example of this took place many years ago when I owned a female Irish Setter. Her name was Dolly, and she and I lived together in a small apartment on Hollywood's

It's a pen full of puppies.

**Part 2**

Sunset Strip. Because I made my living as a freelance writer, I spent all day, every day at home. Dolly was one of the most well-behaved house dogs I have ever owned. She was housetrained in a flash, obedient without question, and a true lady in every respect when we went out for our daily walks along the boulevard.

A close friend was such an admirer of Dolly that he too decided to get an Irish Setter. His Mame came from the same kennel as Dolly, and they both had many ancestors in common. My friend also lived in an apartment. Mame, however, was no Dolly! She couldn't be left alone for more than five minutes without expressing her objection at being "abandoned." Mame pulled up wall-to-wall carpeting, chewed table legs, ate pillows–nothing was safe from her indignation, not even pictures on the wall.

> ### Did You Know?
> There is no breed of dog that cannot be trained. True, some breeds appear to be more difficult to get the desired response from than others. This is more likely due to the trainer not being personality-specific in his or her approach than it is to the dog's inability to learn. With the proper approach, any dog can be taught to be a good canine citizen.

Successful training depends on both the dog and the owner.

Same breed, same ancestors, but yet Mame and Dolly needed entirely different handling and training; something my friend never quite seemed to understand. He was as much to blame (or even more to blame) as his dog for what occurred. The lesson to be learned from this tale is that what works for one dog may not necessarily work for another. And the question for the owner is whether or not you have the patience, energy, and tender loving care that your dog requires to have a healthy relationship with you.

Although there are other factors involved, ease of training depends in great part upon just how much a dog needs his master's approval. The entirely dependent dog lives to please his master and will do everything in his power to evoke the approval response from the person to whom he is devoted. At the opposite end of the spectrum, there is the totally independent dog that is not remotely concerned with what his master thinks. Dependency varies from one dog to the next–even within specific breeds. In the end, successfully training your dog depends upon fully understanding the dog's character and dealing with it accordingly.

## Bonding with Humans

Some professionals who train dogs specifically advise obtaining a puppy at about seven weeks of age. Their research indicates that it is at this precise point in time that a puppy is most ready to bond to a human and subsequently depends upon that person for approval. They believe that prior to that time, the puppy needs to be with his siblings and mother. After that time, the puppy passes through varying stages that lessen the puppy's need to bond with humans and make him more independent in nature. I am not sure that all animal behaviorists would attempt to be this precise; however, there does seem to be general agreement that the optimum time to bring a puppy into his new home is at about seven to eight weeks of age, depending upon the breed. Even so, literally hundreds of thousands of other dogs can be successfully adopted, and you may have already decided that an adult dog is more to your liking.

Choosing an adult dog has both positive and negative aspects. On the positive side, the adult dog's temperament is pretty well set and more easily determined, so you will have some clues as to how your personalities might mesh. A less positive aspect is the fact that the dog may be set in his ways and you will have to work a bit harder to undo habits that do not work for your household.

Puppies look to their owners for approval.

Choose a training method that is appropriate for your dog's needs.

Part 2

Don't adopt any dog, puppy or adult, based simply on the way he looks. Spend as much time as you can with the dog before piling him into your car and rushing him home. Pick an adult dog whose personality matches yours. If you are a laid-back individual who has a low-key approach to life, an excitable, off-the-wall kind of a dog may be more than you can cope with. On the other hand, an extroverted tri-athlete may not find the ideal companion in a pokey, mellow, short-legged dog.

Keeping all of this in mind will give you a more definite and suitable approach to training, rather than having expectations of your dog that he will find extremely difficult, if not impossible, to live up to. Observe the dog you have selected and act accordingly. Do not rush to judgment and mistake your dog's unwillingness to respond for a lack of intelligence. This is probably not the case at all. A better way of viewing your dog's mental capacity may be that he is thinking a lot, thus prolonging his training, which the owner may not always appreciate. On the other hand, while the less "intelligent" breeds may be easier to train, there's many an owner who would not trade the excitement of seeing what his dog will come up with next for all the perfect behavior in the manuals. Life is a tradeoff. Whatever the case, every breed of dog is trainable when you use the best approach for his individual personality.

*Housetraining your puppy should be a positive experience.*

## Paper Training

If you find it necessary to be away from home all day, it does not mean that you cannot successfully housetrain your dog. You will not be able to take your puppy outside for regular walks or leave him in a crate; however, do not make the mistake of allowing him to roam the house or even a large room at will. Begin housetraining your dog by confining him to some out-of-the-way corner that is easily accessible to him. You can choose a small room or an area of the house partitioned with baby gates, and cover the floor with newspaper or puppy pads.

Make your dog's special area large enough so that the he will not have to relieve himself next to his bed, food, or water. You will soon find that your pup will be inclined to

### Pads or Papers?

Although newspapers involve no extra cost, they usually get both the puppy and the area in which he is confined dirty because of the ink smudges, and they don't always absorb what the puppy has to offer. You may want to consider pads instead. They are absorbent, lined to prevent leaks, and some are treated with and attractant to lure your puppy to them when he needs to eliminate.

Crate training is one of the quickest ways to housetrain your dog.

use one particular spot to perform his bowel and bladder functions. When you are home, you must take the dog to this exact spot to eliminate at the appropriate time. If you consistently take your dog to the same spot, you will reinforce the habit of going there for that purpose.

## Crate Training

There is another relatively easy method to housetrain most dogs that works well with both puppies and adults—with little, hot-wired dogs, big subdued dogs, and every kind in between. It's called the cage or crate method, which is based very simply on the fact that the average dog does not like to mess near where he eats and sleeps. I've known first-time dog owners who thought this method of housetraining was cruel initially, but those same people have returned later to thank me for having suggested it in the first place. Interestingly in many cases, dogs will come to think of their crates as their den. All dogs need a place of their own to retreat to and you will probably find that your dog will

### Crate Size

In the case of a puppy, it will not be necessary to dash out and buy a new crate every few weeks to accommodate the puppy's rapid growth spurts. Simply but a large crate and cut a piece of plywood to partition off the excess space, moving it back as needed. I assure you that your puppy will be housetrained long before you have lost the need for the partition.

Part 2

## Crate Time

Naturally, the length of time that the young puppy will be able to contain himself must be taken into consideration. Two or three hours in the crate is the maximum in the beginning, except at night when the entire household is quiet and dark. The length of time can be increased as the puppy grows older. If you ignore the dog when he cries to come out and only let him out when he is being quiet, it will usually get a dog to understand that theatrics will not result in liberation.

consider his cage or crate that place. Wire cages and fiberglass shipping kennels come in varied sizes and can be purchased at your favorite pet emporium. Nylabone makes a Fold-Away Pet Carrier® that can be stored and carried around easily. The cage or crate used for housetraining should be large enough for the dog to stand up, lie down, and stretch out in comfortably, but only that big.

Begin by feeding your dog in the crate. Keep the door closed and latched while he is eating. When the meal is finished, open the crate and, if possible, carry the dog outdoors to the spot where you want him to eliminate. It is important to go back to the same spot each and every time. First, because the dog will get the message that this is the place for doing his "business" more quickly. Second, it will save you hours of clean-up time when droppings need only be collected from one location rather than from all over the yard.

If you are not able to watch your dog every minute, he should be in his cage or crate with the door securely latched. Each time you put your dog inside the crate, give him a small treat. Throw the treat to the back of the crate, and encourage the dog to walk in on his own. When he does, give him lots of praise and perhaps another piece of the treat through the wires of the cage. Do not succumb to your dog's initial complaints about being in his crate. The puppy must learn to stay in his cage and to do so without complaining. If you respond to the puppy's vocal demands to be let out, you are sure to reinforce–you guessed it–barking.

Give your puppy ample time outside while housetraining.

Your puppy will very quickly learn to "voice" every single complaint he may have. This is not only annoying, but you will never be able to determine if there really is a need to go outside.

## Dog Runs

Depending on the size and age of your dog, his amount of coat, and the availability of an outdoor area, you may be able to leave him in a secure run while you are away from home. I would not leave a puppy outdoors alone for long periods, nor would I consider this an option for small or smooth-coated dogs in extreme temperatures. Otherwise, an outdoor run is a good option for the dog that has to stay home alone regularly for more than a few hours at a time. This method not only ensures you that there will be no mistakes made indoors, but also avoids confusing your dog as to where he should and should not relieve himself.

Dog runs allow your dog to exercise while keeping him contained.

Don't misunderstand—this is not to infer that any dog is to be abandoned to the outdoors until he is housetrained. First, the dog will never learn to be clean in the home if he spends little or no time there. Second, denying a dog regular human contact can result in his becoming neurotic and uncontrollable.

## The Watchful Eye

It is important that you do not let puppies loose after eating. Young puppies will eliminate almost immediately after eating or drinking. They will also be ready to relieve themselves when they first wake up and after playing. If you keep a watchful eye on your pup, you will quickly learn when this is about to

Most puppies need to eliminate immediately after eating or drinking.

## Up-And-At Em!

Do not dawdle when you wake up in the morning. Your first priority will be to get your dog outdoors. Just how early this ritual will take place will depend much more on your puppy than on you. If your dog is like most others, there will be no doubt in your mind when he needs to be let out. You will also very quickly learn to tell the difference between the "this-is-an-emergency" complaint and "I-just-want-out" grumbling. Do not test any dog's ability to contain himself. His early morning vocal demand to be let out is confirmation that the housetraining lesson is being learned.

## Accidents

There are some adult dogs that just seem unable to keep from having indoor accidents, and on occasion, dogs that may have been completely housetrained begin to experience difficulty in waiting to go outside. These accidents may be due to medical conditions that your veterinarian can diagnose and successfully treat. If your patience is running short and you have been consistent in your training methods, the problem may not be in your training or in the dog's willingness to be housetrained. Your veterinarian may be able to help considerably.

take place. He usually circles and sniffs the floor just before he relieves himself. Do not give your puppy an opportunity to learn that he can eliminate in the house. Your housetraining chores will be reduced considerably if you avoid bad habits in the first place. If you see him exhibiting signs that he needs to go out, pick him up immediately and take him outside where you want him to go. Praise him when he goes in the correct area so that he knows that this is what you want him to do. Also, while on the subject of avoidance–never underestimate its importance in regard to bad habits. Dr. Ian Dunbar, a highly respected canine behaviorist, strongly cautions against allowing puppies to do anything they choose, even in the first few days they spend in their new homes. He believes this permissiveness sets up a pattern for misbehavior. Once a puppy or dog realizes he can do something, even if you do not approve of what he has done, you have two jobs to do instead of one: You have to teach the dog that the behavior is unacceptable, and then proceed to teach him the proper way to behave.

Understand that a pup of 8 to 12 weeks of age will not be able to contain himself for long periods of time. Puppies of that age must relieve themselves every few hours, except at night. Your schedule must be adjusted accordingly. Also make sure that both puppies and adults have relieved themselves, both bowel and bladder, the last thing at night before going to bed.

## Puppy Preschool

It was once believed that no serious training should be undertaken until dogs were at least eight months old. Some trainers wouldn't consider working with a dog that was less than 12 or 14 months of age. However, the tide began to turn nearly 30 years ago through the research of noted canine behaviorist John Paul Scott. It was found that puppies can learn and can learn well far before the previously recommended ages. In fact, it was discovered that a puppy's most critical period of imprinting is between 3 and 14 weeks of age. Behaviorists began to realize that this time frame was also the most ideal time to mold a puppy's personality.

Puppies can begin training at eight or nine weeks of age.

Today, classes for puppies as young as eight and nine weeks of age are appearing around the country and the results have been nothing but positive. It is now believed that, in general, a dog will be more adaptable and receptive to advanced schooling when training takes place very early in life. Pups that have had the advantage of "preschool" training are continually proving to be more self-assured and able to meet a modern dog's increased social demands without being traumatized. Furthermore, the strange sights, sounds, and the distractions of these early classes are soon taken in stride by the youngster, and he is able to concentrate on the lessons at hand much more easily.

Preschool lessons are not complicated or intense, but many of them will be important throughout the dog's entire life. There is no reason why a puppy cannot learn how to walk along nicely on

Healthy treats can be used as motivational tools in training.

With the right training, your puppy can learn all kind of tricks.

a leash when necessary or understand the meaning of the word "no." It doesn't take a canine wonder to learn simple things like this, and these lessons could also easily save your dog's life.

A thorough understanding of how dogs learn and how they communicate can help you and your pet develop a relationship that far exceeds any that you may have had with dogs in your past. As I have stressed over and over again, no dog, even the most highly trained, will automatically know all the things you will want him to know about living with you. All dogs are born with a clean slate, the writing is put on that slate by their experiences and their owners. It is very important that you write exactly what it is you want on that slate.

## Did You Know?

Dog owners must be aware that all of the things that work best for teaching humans cannot simply be transferred to their dogs. Something that seems entirely reasonable and logical to us will not apply to our dogs because they have an entirely different set of instinctual behaviors and thought processes. If you have an understanding of these instincts before you start, you can build a solid relationship with your dog built on trust and mutual understanding.

# How Dogs Learn

We obey laws because we know that if we don't, dire consequences have been arranged to punish us for our transgressions. We have the ability to conceptualize–to imagine.

Some canine behaviorists think that all dogs' behavior comes from instinct. Others argue that dogs learn in the same rational manner as humans do, or at least as human children do. Both schools of thought are able to offer convincing proof as to the validity of their beliefs. I believe that there is truth in both theories.

One cannot have lived with as many dogs as I have through the years and not observed what is clearly instinctual behavior at times and what is obviously

With the proper training, any dog can become a good canine citizen.

This dog gets a handshake for a job well done.

It's puppy's natural instinct to chase anything that moves.

rational behavior at others. I do believe dogs learn to obey our "laws" in a manner that is similar but different from the way that we do. Because dogs learn differently, we must approach teaching them in a different manner.

## Word Association

A specific word has no real meaning for a dog. A dog will respond to what action he associates with the word. For example, you and I understand what is meant by the words "chocolate sundae"–someone taught us that was the name for a combination of certain sweet things. We also understand that the word "desert" could also mean chocolate sundae or a number of equally appealing things to eat.

This is where we differ from our dogs. Rover understands what "chicken" is because every time we say the word, he gets a piece of chicken. However, asking him if he wants "poultry" means nothing to him. Although Rover may start salivating at the mere mention of the word "chicken," you could substitute the word "hammer" for "chicken," and as long as you use the word "hammer" every time you give Rover a piece of chicken, it would soon mean the same thing.

There are two lessons to be understood here. The first is that dogs can associate a word with a substance or an event (event meaning something like going outside or riding in a car). However, using different words to express the same command, even if the words have the exact same meaning, will only serve to confuse your dog–the connection cannot be made. For example, automobile and car have exactly the same meaning to you and I, but not to our dogs. They can only associate a given word with one result.

## Instinct

All dogs have some instinctive behaviors. This applies whether the dog is a Great Dane, toy Poodle, Golden Retriever, or a combination of all three. The reason for this is that all dogs, regardless of breed, descend from the same source–Canis lupus, the wolf. That distant ancestor contributed certain genes to his descendants that have proven so necessary for a dog's existence that they are still in use. Granted, man has manipulated these hereditary inclinations to suit himself, but most of what dogs do can be traced back to his wolf ancestors.

From this lupine ancestor, most dogs have inherited an instinct to chase. I am fairly sure that, even among the earliest wolves, some were more addicted to and better at chasing than others, and so it has been with their descendants. There are dogs that will chase a ball, a stick, or even the neighbor's cat only if they have nothing else to do. There are also dogs that will chase just about anything that moves–every time it moves! The chasers can be trained not to chase, but you will never be able to quell their desire to chase. The instinct courses heavily through their genetic makeup.

There are other instincts for which the need has been eliminated by the passing of time. Most dogs circle round and round on their bedding before lying down. It is believed that this behavior stems from the time when it was necessary to crush down the underbrush in order to make a comfortable bed for the night. Mother dogs regurgitate food for their puppies. This is carried over from the time when it was the most efficient way of bringing home the day's kill for their hungry pups back at the den.

### Basic Instincts

Female dogs do not read books, nor have they ever attended a Lamaze class, yet they know everything there is to know in respect to the birth and care of their offspring. This is instinctual knowledge. Puppies nurse by instinct. Males are compelled to procreate through instinct. All dogs' behavior can be traced back to an instinct that once helped them survive.

It's all about hugs and kisses for this Dalmatian.

**Part 2**

Basset Hounds usually have an instinct to follow their noses.

No one teaches the modern dog any of these behaviors. These traits are contained within the genetic structure of each and every dog. Some of these traits are of little consequence today, but others conflict with how we want our dogs to behave as pets.

## Rational Learning

As strong as the instinctual drive is, there are few people I know who have spent any quality time with dogs that aren't fully convinced that they can think and make logical conclusions. When I drive down to the end of our country road and turn right to the highway, Raif sits back calmly in his seat, gazes out the window, and is ready to calmly go wherever his chauffeur may take him. However, if I were to turn left from our road, this means but one thing to Raif– beach time! And then it's all I can do to keep him contained.

What causes a dog to rush out into the street and snatch a child from the danger of an oncoming auto? Who told our dogs that bringing us their leash or a toy will inspire a walk or play time? There may be a scientific explanation for this behavior, but then I'm sure there is such an explanation for why humans laugh or cry.

Please don't let a dog's ability to think rationally allow you to believe a dog will always use good judgment. A dog is not going to let his good sense get in the way of instinctual behavior. Don't expect your dog to stop and watch for cars when chasing his ball. His instinct will send him after the ball, traffic or not. It is training that will remind him that he has been taught never to run into the street for any reason.

## Reinforcing Behavior

A dog's concept of good and bad is not the same as a person's understanding of it. For example, a dog has the natural need to eliminate. He doesn't care where he goes–it is his owner that cares. This is why you must reinforce his good behavior. If he relieves himself outside or in his designated area, he gets a treat. You are reinforcing that he did well with a reward. With enough positive reinforcement, he will soon know exactly what he is expected to do.

The only way your dog will learn to avoid breaking a specific rule is if there is a negative consequence every time he breaks or attempts to break that rule. Quite simply, the formula is that breaking rules equals unpleasant consequences and abiding by them results in reward of some kind. This formula is easily understood by any dog. But in order for this to work, the unpleasant experience has to occur every single time the unwanted behavior occurs, and it must occur immediately upon breaking the rule. Being corrected for bad behavior some of the time or later in the day means absolutely nothing to a dog. Negative consequences then become something that happen at random, rather than as a result of having done something specific. Soon your dog will equate good behavior with positive rewards.

Positive reinforcement is a big part of the training process.

Why then do dogs insist upon doing things that will get them into trouble? They may know they will be in trouble when they raid the trash can and scatter the contents over the kitchen floor, but the behavior continues.

This is about satisfying a need. There is no doubt that the dog got some reward–perhaps the last of the prime rib–as a result of his first trash can raid. The next time it happened, the prize was a meaty soup bone. Now you have to think like a dog. Which is worse? Being reprimanded by you later or passing up the gourmet treat just a few nudges of the trash can away? After several successful trash can raids, your dog knows for certain there is a pot of gold under that lid. Forget the scolding! That comes later; the pork chop comes now.

Puppies look to their owners for guidance and discipline.

Part 2

## Avoidance

The more often your dog repeats an undesirable act, the more difficult it will be to remove that behavior from the dog's memory. It is being reinforced. That's why avoidance is a key part of your dog's training. If a dog never has a housetraining accident indoors, you will not have to "untrain" that behavior before you begin to train him to go outdoors. If you do not allow your dog to chase the neighbor's cat, it will make it much easier on all of you (the neighbor, the cat, your dog, and you!) than having to convince him that cat-chasing is not fun.

Remember to use praise in conjunction with your training.

Whose fault is this? Yours! ("Of course," you think, "the parent always gets the blame!") But seriously, one of the most important principles of successful training has been ignored here–avoidance. The trash should not have been made accessible to the dog in the first place. Now the problem behavior is set. And now that the dog has been able to raid the gourmet treasure box for a second and third time, the thrill of victory is worth the agony of getting caught.

There are transgressions that merit correction, but the correction itself must be appropriate. Having your brand new rug chewed to bits or the stuffing pulled out of your sofa isn't exactly funny. However, don't make the mistake of interpreting your dog's actions in human terms. What you may interpret as retaliation on the part of your pet is far more apt to be instinct, or even anxiety and frustration. Although it may appear your dog did something out of sheer spite, it is very important for you to understand that this was not part of some diabolical plan to punish you.

I've had so many people tell me that their dog "pays them back" for being left behind by destroying the most expensive thing they can sink their teeth into. They have entirely misunderstood why their dog did what he did. First, dogs don't know what "expensive" or "valuable" means. Second, the dog simply missed his favorite person and got as close as he could to the loved one in the best way the dog knew how. The owner, of course, has misinterpreted this behavior as retaliation.

Yelling and screaming will only make a bad situation worse, and a dog should never be hit or abused in any way. Because your tirade usually comes well after the fact, the dog is thoroughly confused by your behavior, and physical violence will not only endanger his welfare, but will make him mistrust and resent you. The only way to ensure that this kind of bad behavior will never happen again is to confine your dog to a safe place when you are away from him or if he is unsupervised. If you catch him in the act of doing something wrong, be calm, be fair, and be consistent. Don't punish him for something that he has been permitted to do before or do in another place. A firm, "No!" and the removal of your dog from the situation is all that is needed to get your point across.

This should give you some idea as to why a dog does or doesn't do what we think he should. Understanding how he works his way from A to Z will contribute tremendously to the success you will have in teaching him anything you want him to learn.

Being firm and consistent will yield the best results during training.

# The Basics of Training

It is important for dog owners to remember that the average dog thrives when learning new things. Your dog has a great capacity to learn, and the best training tip I can offer the new owner is to proceed with lots of patience and perform many repetitions of the command. If your dog is learning easily and then suddenly won't do anything for you, go back one step in the training and retrain before going forward.

## The Come Command

The most important lesson for any dog to learn is to come when called. Many trainers believe that your dog's knowledge of this command is central to everything else that will eventually be taught to him. Learning to come teaches the dog that you are in

Every dog can benefit from basic training.

## Practice Makes Perfect

Training lessons should take place every day, but for short periods of time. Dogs can become bored when pressed too long or too hard and will often shut down completely. Training sessions of a few minutes several times a day are ideal. Training should never take place when you are irritated, distressed, or preoccupied, nor should you begin basic training in crowded or noisy places because the distractions may interfere with you or your dog's concentration. Once the commands are understood and learned, you can begin testing your dog in public places, but at first the two of you should work somewhere you can concentrate fully upon each other

command–you are the ultimate authority that must always be obeyed.

I recommend always using the command with the dog's name. Therefore, it is very important that even a very young puppy learn his name as soon as possible. Constant repetition of the pup's name usually does the trick. Use his name every time you speak to him. "Want to go outside, Lad?" "Come, Lad, come!"

## Did You Know?

It will take a bit of doing to control your anger when Fido refuses to come when called. Dogs are capable of detecting anger in your voice even though you may be outwardly pretending to be in the best of spirits.

As I've said before and will repeat again, it is much easier to avoid the establishment of bad habits than it is to correct them once set. Avoid giving the come command at all costs unless you are sure your puppy will come to you. The very young pup is far more inclined to respond to learning the come command than the older dog that is less dependent on you.

Learning to come on command could save your dog's life when the two of you venture out into the world. The come command must be obeyed without question, but it should represent nothing but positive things in the dog's mind. It is your duty to help the dog associate the word with life's pleasantries–praises, pats, treats, and you, of course. He should never associate this command with fear. All too often, novice trainers get very angry at their dogs for not responding immediately to the come command. When the dog finally does come or gets caught by the owner after a chase, the owner scolds him for not obeying. The dog then begins to associate the word "come" with an unpleasant result.

Use the command initially when the puppy is already on his way to you or give the command while walking or running away from the youngster. Clap your hands and sound very happy and excited about having him join in on this "game." The very young dog will normally want to stay as close to his owner as possible, especially in strange surroundings. When your puppy sees you moving away, his natural inclination will be to get close to you. This is a perfect time to use the come command.

Later, as a puppy grows more self-confident and independent, you may want to attach a long leash or rope to his collar to ensure the correct response. Again, do not chase or punish your puppy for not obeying the come command. Doing so in the initial stages of training makes the youngster associate the command with punishment, and this will result in avoidance rather than the immediate positive response you desire. It is imperative that you praise your pup and give him a treat when he does come to you, even if he purposely delays responding for many minutes.

Be sure that you repeat this command in exactly the same way every time you expect the dog to respond to it. Don't say, "Come, Shep, come," one time and "Here boy," the next. It's just as if someone asked you to do something in English one time, in Swahili the next, and in Martian the time after that. Be consistent in the way you ask your dog to do something, and, in no time, he will consistently obey.

## Leash Training

It is never too early to accustom your puppy to a collar and leash. It is your way of keeping your dog under control. It may not be necessary for the puppy or adult dog to wear his collar and identification tags within the

This Saint puppy gets a little help learning the sit command.

Patience and consistency are the keys to successful training.

*Treats and praise can help motivate your dog during training.*

### Leash Lessons

If your pup is the one that needed special treatment to get the leash lesson under way and is wearing the leash as a shoulder strap, wait until your walks are taken in stride before making any changes. You can then start attaching the leash to his collar, and chances are that there will no longer be any resistance.

confines of your home, but no dog should ever leave home without a collar on and without the leash held securely in your hand.

Begin getting your dog or puppy accustomed to his collar by leaving it on for a few minutes at a time, gradually extending the time you leave it on. Most dogs become accustomed to a collar very quickly and forget they are even wearing one. Once this is accomplished, attach a lightweight leash to the collar while you are playing with him. Do not try to guide him at first. The point here is to accustom the pup to the feeling of having something attached to the collar.

Some puppies adapt to a collar very quickly and, without any undo resistance, learn to be guided with the leash. Other pups may be absolutely adamant that they will not have any part of leash training and seem intent on strangling themselves before submitting.

If your puppy is one of the latter, do not continue to force the issue. Simply create a lasso with your leash and put your puppy's head and front legs through the lasso opening so that the leash encircles his shoulders and chest, just behind the front legs. Problem pups seem to object less to this method than having the leash around their necks. Encourage your puppy to follow you as you move away. If he is reluctant to cooperate, coax him along with a treat of some kind. Hold the treat in front of his nose to encourage him to follow you. Just as soon as your puppy takes a few steps toward you, praise him enthusiastically and continue to do so as you move along.

Make the initial session very brief and enjoyable. Continue the lesson until the puppy is completely unconcerned about the fact that he is on a leash. With a treat in one hand and a leash in the other, you can begin to use both to guide him in the direction you wish to go.

## The No Command

One of the most important commands your puppy will ever learn is the meaning of the word "no." It is critical that the puppy learns this command just as soon as possible. Understanding that the command must be obeyed instantly could save your dog's life.

Running off and becoming lost, chasing a child or another animal into the road, or picking up and eating a harmful substance are not beyond the average dog's behavior. Being able to stop the action instantly is obviously important in these situations and using the word "no" is the shortest, quickest way to do so.

One important piece of advice in using this and all other commands—never give a command that you are not prepared and able to enforce. The only way a puppy learns to obey commands is to realize that once issued, commands must be complied with. Learning the no command should start on the first day of the puppy's arrival at your home.

## The Sit and Stay Commands

The sit and stay commands are just as important to your dog's safety (and your sanity!) as the no command and learning to come when called. Even the very youngest preschool puppies learn the sit command

Every dog needs to understand and obey the no command.

The sit command is the foundation for all other commands.

Part 2

quickly, especially if it appears to be a game and a food treat is involved. Your pup should always be on his collar and leash for lessons. Young puppies, even grown dogs for that matter, are not beyond getting up and walking away when they have decided that you and your lessons are boring.

As in most cases with dogs, a food treat always seems to get the lesson across to the student. By placing a food treat in front of the dog, raising it over his head, and telling him to sit, the dog will most likely sit automatically as he follows the treat. If he accomplishes this, praise him lavishly and give him the treat as a reward. If this doesn't work, give the sit command immediately before lightly pushing down on your dog's hindquarters or gently scooping the hind legs from under him, molding him into a sit position. Praise your dog when he does sit, even though it is you who made the action take place. Continue holding the dog's rear end down and repeat the sit command several times. If your dog makes an attempt to get up, repeat the command yet again while exerting light pressure on the rear end until the correct position is assumed. A treat given as a reward will make him eager to repeat the command. Make your dog stay in this position for increasing lengths of

The stay command is useful during grooming procedures.

### Puppy Limits

Only when you decide your dog should get up should he be allowed to do so. Do not test the limits of a very young puppy's patience. Remember that you are dealing with a baby. The attention span of any youngster, canine or human, is relatively short. When you do decide your pup can get up, call his name, say "Okay," and make a big fuss over him. Praise and a food treat are in order every time your puppy responds correctly.

time. Begin with a few seconds and increase the time as your lesson progresses over the following weeks. If your young student attempts to get up or to lie down, he should be corrected by simply saying, "Sit!" in a firm voice. This should be accompanied by returning the dog to the desired position.

Once he has mastered the sit lesson, you may start on the stay command. With your dog on leash and facing you, command him to sit, then take a step or two back. If your dog attempts to get up to follow you, firmly say, "Sit, stay!" While you are saying this, raise your hand, palm toward the dog, and again command, "Stay!" Any attempt on your dog's part to get up must be corrected at once, returning him to the sit position and repeating, "Stay!" Once your dog begins to understand what you want, you can gradually increase the distance you step back. With a long leash attached to your dog's collar (even a clothesline will do), start with a few steps and gradually increase the distance to several yards. Your dog must eventually learn that the sit and stay commands must be obeyed no matter how far away you are. Later on, with advanced training, your dog will learn that the command is to be obeyed even when you move entirely out of sight.

As your dog masters this lesson and is able to remain in the sit position for as long as you dictate, avoid calling the dog to you at first. This makes the dog overly anxious to get up and run to you. Instead, walk back to your dog and say, "Okay," which is a signal that the command is over. When your dog becomes more reliable in this respect, you can call him to you. The sit/stay lesson can take a considerable amount of your time and patience, especially with a puppy, because of his short attention span. In the case of young puppies, don't make the stay part of the lesson go on forever. Everything in a very young dog's makeup urges him to stay close to you wherever you go. Forcing him to operate against his natural instincts can be bewildering to the dog.

This Pembroke Welsh Corgi gets rewarded for a job well done.

**Part 2**

Be sure to associate the down command with positive rewards.

### Reward Down

Because "Down" can have a negative association to your dog, it is important that you do everything you can to associate the command with as many positive rewards as possible. Food treats help a lot, as does enough praise to make the dog think he is just wonderful.

## The Down Command

Once your dog has mastered the sit and stay commands, you may begin work on the down command. This is the single-word command for lie down. Use the down command only when you want the dog to lie down. If you want your dog to get off your sofa or to stop jumping up on people, use the off command. Do not interchange these two commands. Doing so will only confuse your dog, after which evoking the right response will become next to impossible. The down position is especially useful if you want your dog to remain in a particular place for a long period of time. A dog is usually far more inclined to stay put when he is lying down than when he is sitting. Teaching this command may take more time and patience than the previous lessons. It is believed by some animal behaviorists that assuming the down position somehow represents submissiveness to the dog. It's all a part of canine body language.

Begin with your dog sitting in front of and facing you. Hold a treat in your right hand with the excess part of the leash in your left hand. Bring the treat under the dog's nose and slowly move your hand down to the ground. Your dog will follow the treat with his head and neck. As he does, give the command, "Down," and exert light pressure on his shoulders with your left hand. If your dog resists the pressure on his shoulders, do not continue pushing down. Doing so will only create more resistance.

An alternative method of getting your dog headed into the down position is to move around to the dog's right side, and as you draw his attention downward with your right hand, place your left hand or arm under the dog's front legs and gently slide them forward. In the case of a very young dog or puppy, you will undoubtedly have to be on your knees next to the youngster. As your dog's forelegs begin to slide out to the front, keep moving the treat along the ground until the dog's whole body is lying down while continuing to repeat, "Down." Once he has assumed the position you desire, give him the treat and a lot of praise. Continue assisting your dog into the down position until he does so on his own. Be firm, be patient, and be prepared for those occasional "I have no idea what you mean" looks your dog student may give you.

## The Heel Command

Having your dog heel simply means that your dog will walk on your left side with his shoulder next to your leg on a loose leash. The dog will do this no matter which direction you might go or how quickly you turn. Teaching your dog to heel is really important because it will not only make your daily walks far more enjoyable, it will make for a far more tractable companion when the two of you are in crowded or confusing situations. I can't tell you how often I see people being pulled down the street in all but a flat-out horizontal position behind their dog. There is no reason for this to be going on, and mastering the heel command will help prevent this from happening.

### Did You Know?

You may want to begin the heel lesson a few steps at a time. Three or four steps at a time without pulling on the lead are three or four steps in the right direction. Take those pull-free steps, have your dog sit, and praise him to the high heavens. It is a good idea to change from the collar your dog normally wears to a special training collar constructed in a manner that will assist in the training. There are many different kinds of collars that can be purchased.

Teaching your dog to heel will make your daily walks more enjoyable.

Choose a collar that best fits your breed of dog.

### Equipment
### Buckle Collars

Made of leather, cloth, or woven nylon, this collar is manufactured on the same principle as a belt for pants. It is fine for a very small dog or for one that responds to slightest pull, but by and large, its value is limited for training purposes.

### Head Halter

A head halter fits the dog's entire head and is particularly useful when handling dogs that can be aggressive with other animals. It gives the trainer the added advantage of being able to turn the dog's head when necessary.

### Chain-Link Collar

I particularly recommend a lightweight, chain-link training collar for the heeling lesson. It provides both quick pressure around the neck and a snapping sound, both of which get the dog's attention.

To put the chain-link collar on your dog properly, slip one loop of the chain through one of the rings at the end of the collar. Lay the collar down on a flat surface and create the

Give your pet time to get used to the unfamiliar feel of a collar.

### No Choking!

Some trainers call the Chain-Link collar a "choke collar." I don't like that name and never use it, because when the link-chain collar is used properly, it does not choke the dog, nor was it ever intended to be used in this manner.

Part 2

## Dog Owners Beware

Do not leave the chain-link collar on your dog when training sessions are finished. Some dogs are ingenious at getting their lower jaw or legs caught in the training collar and could seriously hurt themselves if you aren't around. Also, changing to the chain-link collar at training time signals to your dog that this is all business and it is time get serious.

Be sure to remove your dog's collar after each training session.

letter "P" with the chain. Pick the collar up by sliding your right hand through the loop of the "P." With your dog facing you, hold his muzzle with your right hand and let the collar slip over his head and down around his neck. You can then snap the leash on to the free ring of the collar.

The chain-link collars are constructed of metal links that are graduated in size, depending on the size of the collar. The smallest collars are made of links that are practically mesh, while the collars suitable for large- or giant-sized dog are made of rugged and sturdy chains.

Take your dog along with you when you shop for this collar. Your pet supply source will then be able to advise you which collar would be most suitable for your dog and the proper way to put it on.

When you begin training your puppy or grown dog to walk along on the leash, you should accustom him to walking on your left side. The leash should cross your body from the dog's collar to your right hand. The excess portion will be folded into your right hand, and your left hand will be used to make corrections with the leash.

All training sessions should be conducted in an area free of distractions.

Training should be fun and rewarding for both dog and owner.

A quick, short snap of the leash with your left hand will keep your dog from lunging from side to side, pulling ahead, or lagging back. As you make a correction, give the heel command. Keep the leash slack as long as your dog maintains the proper position at your side.

If your dog begins to drift away, give the leash a jerk and guide him back to the correct position giving the heel command. Do not pull on the lead with steady pressure. What is needed is an insistent but gentle jerking motion to get his attention. Once your dog gets the hang of it, you can practice turning and walking at different speeds. Your daily walks should be much more enjoyable for both you and your dog.

## Training Classes

There are few limits to what a patient, consistent dog owner can teach his or her dog. If you choose to go beyond the basics to advanced obedience work, you may want to consider local professional assistance. Professional trainers have had long-standing experience in avoiding the pitfalls of obedience training and can help you from making common mistakes.

Most dog owners train their pets at home in the privacy of their backyard or garden. They are later upset to find that their well-trained dog cares not one iota about obeying when strange people and dogs are present.

All too often, beginning trainers read several books about training techniques and try to apply the principles gleaned from all of them. Sometimes this works, but more often than not, it confuses both dog and owner. Staying with one trainer and following his program to its completion will reap greater rewards.

Training assistance can be obtained in many ways. Classes are particularly good for your dog's socialization and attentiveness. Your dog will learn that he must obey—even when there are other dogs and people around to provide temptation. There are free-of-charge classes at many parks and recreation facilities, as well as very formal and sometimes very expensive individual lessons with private trainers. Your veterinarian may have lists of classes and where they take place, or your local pet emporium may hold classes, so it is wise to check these places if you are unable to find what you are looking for on your own.

## Professional Trainers

If you find you are unable to give your dog the kind of training he should have in an effective manner, you may decide to find a private trainer to assist you. When you begin to investigate the situation, you will probably find that there are nearly as many dog trainers as there are dogs to be trained. Like dancers and athletes, there is a wide range of innate talent and ability among trainers. If you are going to go through all the effort and expense of using a professional, make sure you get a good one. Don't get carried away with promises of things like "Three Days to a Perfect Dog," or assurances that your pooch will push Lassie aside for the annual canine acting awards. Good trainers take as much time as each dog requires to learn his lesson. That time frame varies from dog to dog. Credentials speak louder than promises, and so do recommendations from people who have used the trainer. Ask for both. If the trainer

### Obedience School

There are some obedience schools that will take your dog and train him for you. However, unless your schedule provides no time at all to train your own dog, having someone else train him for you would be last on the list of recommendations. The rapport that develops between the owner who has trained his or her own dog to be a pleasant companion and good canine citizen is very special—well worth the time and patience it requires to achieve.

Consult a professional trainer if you are having difficulty training your dog.

appears insulted that you've asked–go elsewhere. An accomplished trainer is proud of what he or she has achieved and even prouder of the students that have successfully graduated.

Be realistic about what you hope a trainer will do for you. A good trainer knows the task at hand is to teach you how to train your dog. You can send him away to a school where the training takes place, but if you haven't learned the proper way to deal with your own dog, all the training lessons in the world will be a waste of time and money.

# Advanced Training

An obedient dog is a joy to have around. Dogs that have had no training are a royal pain the neck! As much as I love dogs, visiting someone whose dog has never been taught to obey is not my idea of fun. Training is necessary for your dog to be accepted into society and for your own sanity. It can take care of the behavior basics, but even beyond that, training can also be a wonderful hobby. With practice, almost any dog and owner can participate, and the classes and competition are offered in and around cities throughout the United States.

The American Kennel Club (AKC) and the United Kennel Club (UKC), the two registry systems here in the United States, have both acknowledged the

Having an energized and positive attitude is conducive to training.

A well-socialized puppy is accepting of strangers.

## Happy Owner, Happy Dog

Your emotional state is just as important to your dog's training as his state of mind at the time. Never begin training when you are irritated, distressed, or distracted. Imagine how difficult it would be to learn something if you were sitting in a classroom and the instructor was thinking about everything else but the lesson at hand. You might gain something from the lesson, but you would surely have learned a great deal more if the instructor had his mind on his work.

benefits of obedience training by offering competitions in which your dog can earn titles and championships. These events range from the somewhat informal Canine Good Citizen™ program to the complex and highly respected obedience degrees involving tracking and scent discrimination.

### Canine Good Citizen™ Program (CGC)

The AKC sponsors this program, which is aimed at making all dogs that graduate from it respected members of the community. Classes geared toward training the handler to qualify his or her dog are offered in most communities. Information about where these classes are conducted can be obtained from the place you shop for your dog's food and supplies, from local kennel clubs, or from the classified section of your newspaper. The CGC is not a competition of any kind–the dog is scored only on his ability to master the basic requirements.

## Did You Know?

The AKC's Canine Good Citizen™ program is not restricted to purebred dogs. All dogs, regardless of their heritage, are eligible, and this certificate just might be the first step you and your dog take on the way to a whole array of obedience titles.

Anyone interested in this program can obtain information regarding rules as well as when and where testing is held directly from the American Kennel Club.

Part 2

# The CGC™ Test

There are ten parts to the CGC test, and the dog has to pass all ten in order to receive the CGC Certificate. The parts are:

1. Appearance and grooming: The dog must be clean, healthy and well-groomed.

2. Acceptance of a friendly stranger: The dog is required to allow a friendly stranger to approach and speak to the handler.

3. Walking on a loose leash: The dog has to walk along attentively next to the handler.

4. Walking through a crowd: The dog is required to walk along, paying attention to the handler without interfering with other people or dogs.

5. Sit and down on command and stay in place: The dog has to respond to each of the handlers commands—sit, down, and stay.

6. Come when called: After being put in a sit or down position ten feet away, the dog must return to the handler when called.

7. Sit while touched by a stranger: A friendly stranger must be able to pet the dog.

8. Positive reaction to another dog: The dog has to keep his attention on the handler, even in the presence of another dog.

9. Calm reaction to distracting sights or noises: These distractions can be an unusual or loud noise or sight of a bicycle or unusual-looking object.

10. Supervised separation: The dog must wait calmly, on a leash, while owner is out of sight for three minutes.

## Obedience and Conformation

Obedience trials are held at both championship shows and at matches, as are the conformation events. The same informal entry procedures that apply to conformation matches apply to obedience as well. The championship or sanctioned obedience trials are usually held in conjunction with conformation events.

Obedience training classes are definitely prerequisites here, because competition is highly precise and based entirely on the dog performing a set series of exercises. The exercises required in

This Basenji effortlessly flies over the high jump.

There are many obedience titles that Your dog can earn.

Participating in competitions can be fun for both dog and owner.

## Obedience Titles

The competition levels, what they include, and corresponding degrees are:

**Novice—Earning a Companion Dog title (CD):**

1. Heel on leash and figure 8
2. Stand for examination
3. Heel free
4. Recall
5. Long sit—one minute
6. Long down—three minutes.

**Open—Earning the Companion Dog Excellent title (CDX)**

1. Heel off leash and figure 8
2. Drop on recall
3. Retrieve on flat
4. Retrieve over high jump
5. Broad jump
6. Long sit—three minutes (with owner out of sight)
7. Long down—five minutes (with owner out of sight).

**Utility—Earning the Utility Dog (UD) degree:**

1. Signal exercise
2. Scent discrimination-Article 1
3. Scent discrimination-Article 2
4. Directed retrieve
5. Moving stand and examination
6. Directed jumping.

Those super dogs that have earned their Utility Dog titles are eligible to go on to compete for the next highest award—the Obedience Trial Championship (OTCh.).

the various classes of competition range from the basics like heel, sit, and lie down in the novice class through the sophisticated exercises of the utility and tracking levels that require scent discrimination and directed jumping.

Each level has a title that can be earned after attaining qualifying scores at a given number of shows.

## Tracking

Tracking events have become very popular among dog owners, and many dogs earn the rare Tracking Dog (TD) and Tracking Dog Excellent titles (TDX). A newer competition called Variable Surface Tracking (VST) is open to the dogs that have won their TD or TDX titles. When the competitors in this category have attained the qualifying scores, they earn the VST designation.

Participating in organized events can be fun for both dog and owner. With a good training foundation, who knows how far your dog can go?

Competition gives your dog the opportunity to show off his natural talents.

Tracking allows your dog to use his natural ability in the performance ring.

# Solving Problems

What my parents assured me were "the best days of my life" (and no doubt the most costly days of their lives!) were spent as an English Education major at Michigan State University. The battle hymn of the teaching staff at MSU at the time was quite simply, "If the learner hasn't learned, the teacher hasn't taught." Most schools of canine behavior are inclined to agree with that principle.

Dogs are smart and can learn quickly–if they are taught properly. Think of your dog as an empty slate. If you want writing to appear there, you are going to have to do it, especially if you want the words to be those that you'll approve of.

At the same time, that doesn't mean that everything

With the correct training and guidance, your dog can learn anything.

## Leader of the Pack

If a young puppy cannot find his pack leader in his owner, he assumes the role of pack leader himself. If there are no rules imposed, the puppy learns to make his own rules. And, unfortunately, the unaware owner continually reinforces the puppy's decisions by allowing these situations to take place. With small dogs, these scenarios can quickly produce a neurotic nuisance. In the case of dogs at the top of the size scale, the result can be downright danger-ous. Neither situation is an acceptable one.

a dog does wrong reflects a flaw on your part. A dog comes equipped with a whole set of instinctual behaviors. Some of those behaviors are acceptable in human society, but a good many of them aren't and must be redirected. But let's back up a bit. Let's go back to a few weeks after your dog was born. Individual breed characteristics aside, all dogs, wild or domesticated, are looking for two things when they leave the nest: a pack leader and the rules set down by the leader by which all members of the pack must abide. Because puppies are cuddly and cute, a good many owners fail miserably in supplying these basic needs. Instead, the owner immediately begins to respond to demands of the adorable little puppy. For example, a pup quickly learns he will be allowed into the house if he is barking or whining, whereas he should be taught that he may only enter the house when he is not barking or whining. A grown dog scratches at the door to come in until the wood begins to wear away. In desperation, the owner allows the dog to enter. This dog has learned that the quickest way to gain admittance is to start scratching a hole. Instead of allowing this unwanted "let me in" behavior to become established in the first place, you must develop a procedure that the dog understands. Before letting him in or out, teach him he must first sit quietly. Then and only then will you open the door. Use this procedure the first time the two of you go out, and you will be amazed at how rapidly your dog learns that sitting quietly at the door gets him just what he wants. In situations of this kind, it is important to make sure the dog learns that the desired behavior has earned him what he wants. Once your dog has accomplished the positive behavior, praise him and then allow him to enter.

As discussed earlier, the key to successful training lies in establishing the proper relationship between dog and owner. The owner or the owning family must be the pack leader, and the individual or family must provide the rules by which the dog abides without exception.

## Dominance

There are a good many ways to establish and maintain leadership with your dog. Some dogs, particularly those that might be considered "guard dog" breeds, have a natural instinct to defend themselves if attacked. This is purely a natural instinct. However, some of these dogs may be inclined to fend off attacks by establishing their dominance and becoming aggressive.

Manhandling and punishing a dog of this nature only exacerbates the problem; the dog is in a self-protecting, aggressive mood, and your attack only intensifies his mood. This is one of the reasons why those who truly understand the more assertive dogs constantly preach the value of obedience training. Punishment will not control aggressiveness in a situation like this. The dog may well return your "attack" by attacking you!

Petting and trying to soothe the dog will not help the situation either. He may take your soothing actions to mean approval for his behavior. You must put the dog under your authority by having him obey your command. This makes him submit to you. Responding to the down command puts the dog in a passive role rather than challenging or encouraging his unwanted behavior. If you have ever watched nature films on television, there is no doubt you noticed who ate first when the pack brought down a kill–it was the pack leader. If your dog eats his evening meal about the same time as you have your dinner, make it a point to eat first and then put your dog's food dish down.

It's important that you establish yourself as your dog's leader.

Your dog should be able to obey your hand signals without difficulty.

Part 2

**Part 2**

## Belly Rubs

Those belly rubs your dog enjoys can serve a good purpose. The only way a dog can get a thoroughly good tummy rub is to lie on his back. This just happens to be a passive posture and a good one to get your dog to become accustomed.

Some dogs are most anxious to please the pack leader, and other dogs don't care if they please him or not. In the wild, dogs of the latter classification are likely to enter into battle with the pack leader for dominance. This seldom happens in the human/canine relationship, but do note that I said seldom and not never. It's easy to see where the "I don't care" kind of dogs can develop problem behaviors. However, even the more dependent dog can sometimes manifest behavior that will drive an owner up the wall.

### Aggression

Most types of aggression can be dealt with and controlled as previously described. In the rare case of unprovoked and uncontrollable rage, however, immediate and drastic measures may have to be taken. The best course of action is to get a professional involved immediately.

As explained in a good many cases, aggression is more likely to be the result of an effort to establish dominance or to be protective. Boundaries, both behavioral and territorial, are very important for dogs to learn. Being taught early on what

A soothing belly rub will relax any dog.

## Did You Know?

Aggression is the most common behavior complaint that dog owners have. It is an umbrella term, and it includes behavior of many different types. Furthermore, some breeds were developed to be aggressive and even dogs of mixed breeding can inherit this trait from dogs in their ancestry. Training can help curb these inherent aggressive tendencies.

## Puppy Behavior

Never select a pup that appears suspicious or hostile. All puppies should have sunny, amiable temperaments, even in breeds bred specifically as guard dogs. The protective part of a dog's nature does not develop until he begins to mature and even then, it should be carefully curbed and directed by the owner.

Basic obedience skills are necessary for good behavior.

**Part 2**

he can and cannot do leaves a dog with aggressive inclinations no opportunity to decide how to behave. It is up to the owner to establish the boundaries by which his or her canine companion will live.

Some dogs take their responsibility to protect too far and inadvertently create problem situations. They feel like they have to defend what they believe to be their territory and, lacking guidance from their owners, establish their own boundaries. Aggressiveness is a natural part of some dogs' personalities. It must be nipped in the bud and redirected when it begins, and if it continues to be a problem, professional help must be obtained at once.

Absolutely no law-abiding citizen should have to endure being menaced by an aggressive dog. Even dogs that were specifically obtained to protect one's family or property must be trained to know their boundaries clearly.

If a dog less than six months of age snaps and bites, it strongly indicates inherited bad temperament. Correcting or harnessing inherited bad temperament is a risky undertaking at best and usually leads to dire consequences at some point in the dog's life. Temperamentally untrustworthy puppies grow up to be temperamentally untrustworthy and dangerous adults.

If the puppy was purchased from a breeder, he should be returned to the breeder without delay. If the puppy has not been obtained from a responsible source, I strongly advise discussing the problem with your veterinarian, who may advise you to see a dog behaviorist.

If the puppy had a sunny disposition growing up, but has begun to display aggressive tendencies at maturity, it is more likely to be an indication of a lack of proper training. Again, only one of you can be in charge. If your dog realizes he can behave as he chooses and is inclined toward aggressiveness, you have a dangerous situation on your hands. Proper training and the establishment of definite boundaries will help to control this type of behavior.

## Separation Blues

Separation blues is a very common problem that occurs when dogs are frequently left alone. In the milder cases, it can be the result of boredom, and reactions can range in intensity from whimpering to constant barking and howling. Extreme cases can lead to downright neurotic and destructive behavior, like hysterical barking and destroying furniture. Some dogs go so far as to relieve themselves throughout the home. These more extreme behaviors are usually associated with a somewhat serious condition called separation anxiety, which we will give special attention to later in this chapter.

Howling or barking while the master is gone is best dealt with by using the handy crate you have for your dog. Keep the crate in the same room with you while you are attending to some project that will take a bit of time. Talk to your dog in a calming voice and in so doing, reassure him that everything is fine.

Begin your absences by walking out of the room for just a minute or so. Gradually increase the time you are gone. When you return, praise the dog in a calm voice or give him a treat. Leaving some article that smells of you will help

Separation problems could be a result of boredom.

## Quiet Time

If your dog or puppy refuses to stay alone without creating major sound effects, begin correcting the behavior by crating the dog in the same room with you. Have the crate in a location where the dog can see you. If the dog begins to whimper to be released, slap your hand down hard on the top of the crate and command, "Quiet!" Nine times out of ten, the abrupt noise will startle the dog into, at least, brief silence. Once he is quiet, praise him for being so good. Doing this once probably won't permanently correct the problem, so you'll have to be adamant about repeating the performance every time your dog lets out even a squeak.

Dogs love to be in the company of their owners.

**Part 2**

comfort the dog when you are away, and a Rhino™ toy stuffed with peanut butter will keep your dog's attention on the goodie rather than on your absence. Fretting and complaining are reduced considerably, if not entirely eliminated, when your dog is getting plenty of exercise; a dog with a high level of pent-up energy is far more likely to think of ways to act out or misbehave.

Here again, insisting your dog learns that lying down or sitting quietly is what leads to release is very effective. This is taught in the same way you had your dog learn the proper way of gaining admittance to a room or into the house.

Some dogs are fine as long as they can see you. It's your absence that launches the vocal tirade. If this is the case, walk in and out of the room several times and extend your absences gradually. Just as soon as the dog begins to complain, rush back in and repeat the rap on the crate as you give the quiet command.

Some of the truly stubborn complainers require more drastic measures. By drastic measures, I mean the tried-and-true spray bottle or what I call the "rattle can" method. The scenario remains the same, except when the dog complains about your absence from the room, rush back and give the dog a good shot of water from the steady stream cycle of your spray bottle. This method seems to be very effective with even the most stubborn offender.

Many dogs are fine indoors but resent being left outdoors. If this is the case, the rattle-can approach might work best. I use an empty aluminum soft drink can and drop a small handful of pennies into it. Shaking this makes a surprisingly loud clatter. When your dog begins to bark, throw the can at the fence or on the ground near him. If possible, do not let him see you throw the can. Lead him to believe that his noise caused the commotion.

These treatments are usually very effective. But then again, some dogs are more persistent than others, and it is up to you to be unwavering in your dedication to the task. Above all, you must have the last word. Never release the dog because he is barking or howling. Release can only come when he is doing what you demand, never because he complained long enough or loud enough.

NYlabones® are a safe way to keep your dog occupied when you are not home.

### Separation Anxiety

Separation anxiety is a problem of a more serious nature and is the result of the dog's fear of being left alone. It is not spiteful behavior, but rather the dog reacting to his fear in a frenzied manner. This problem is emotionally based and can be a difficult one to correct without assistance. There are new drugs that have been approved to help relieve the high anxiety that separation creates. They act on the dog in a manner similar to the calming effective of antidepressants on humans. These drugs can be obtained by prescription through your veterinarian. Although the medication does not actually cure the problem, it relieves the symptoms to the extent that retraining can begin.

Another dog or even a cat, if the two are compatible, may often solve an anxiety problem immediately, while other dogs respond well to something as simple as having the radio playing while you are gone.

A dog that reacts to loneliness by being destructive should never be allowed to remain loose when you are gone. Some people think it is cruel to confine their dog to an area or a crate where he is not able to destroy things, but they think nothing of becoming furious and frightening the dog out of his wits when he has been free to be destructive. Your reacting in a rage will only tend to enforce the dog's fear of being alone.

Regardless of the cause–loneliness or separation anxiety–the problem is compounded by owners who make their departures and returns appear to be monumental events. Don't upset your dog before leaving by giving the poor fellow hugs and kisses like you are ready to take off on a year-long safari. Just go! When you return, don't make it a climax suitable for the theater screen. Some dogs love those dramatic returns and begin vocally requesting them the minute you walk out the door. Make leaving home and coming home as uneventful as possible or distract your dog by offering him a toy or treat before you leave. If he is happily occupied, chances are he won't even notice you've gone.

## Housetraining Problems

My best advice is simply not to give your dog the opportunity to make mistakes in the house. If the dog is paper- or puppy-pad trained, there is no reason he should be allowed to eliminate anywhere else but the specific spot you have directed him to.

In order to survive those first few weeks of puppyhood with a dog that needs housetraining, I set about teaching him to "tell" me when he wants to go outdoors. When I know the youngster is able to hold onto what he has to do outdoors for a bit, I start asking, "Outside, Rex?" Eventually, I get some reaction–a squeak or a sneeze, etc. With that, I praise the dog like he has just recited a flawless rendition of the Gettysburg Address and out the door we fly.

*Your dog's body language will let you know when he needs to go outside.*

Sooner or later, in anticipation of being let outdoors (or perhaps of being praised), Rex will

Part 2

Monitoring Your dog's water intake can help control his need to eliminate.

## Free Feeding

Free feeding is fine for some dogs, but not for all. Grown dogs that are having problems getting the housetraining message should only be fed at regular meal times and then confined until they can be taken to the place where they should eliminate. Once you are satisfied that their business has been taken care of, you can allow them a reasonable amount of freedom. But if you can't watch your dog, the crate or a safe, confined area is the place for him.

## Did You Know?

If housetraining is proving to be a problem or if your puppy or young dog is having problems containing himself overnight, there are measures you can take that will help. If urinating is the problem, restrict water after 6:00 or 7:00 pm. If bowel movements are taking place at night, give the final meal of the day at an earlier time. In any event, make sure the pup is taken outdoors or to his designated area just before you retire for the evening.

heighten the sound effects with a good sharp bark. As time marches along, my dogs will usually come to me when the need arises, and they let me know in no uncertain vocal terms that it is indeed "time to go out!"

If urinating indoors is a problem, you might try controlling the availability of water. Make it available often, but only at certain times throughout the day. Put the water bowl down and then keep an eye on what is going on. Puppies usually will have to relieve themselves within a few minutes of drinking. Adults will usually have to do so in about a half hour or so.

Frequent urinating of small amounts or chronic diarrhea could mean intestinal or urinary tract problems. Consult your veterinarian without delay.

### Leg Lifting

This may be confusing to new dog owners, but when a male marks his turf, it has absolutely nothing to do with

## Wandering

Normally, this is mostly a male problem. Females are ready to breed twice a year—a male is ready any time and will shop around to see if there are any ladies in waiting. Again, neutering can help solve the wandering problem, but there is absolutely no better insurance against this than a securely fenced yard.

*Putting up a baby gate will prevent your dog from wandering.*

whether or not he is housetrained. Adult males have a natural instinct to lift their legs and urinate to "mark" their home territory. Home territory to a dog includes everything you own–furniture, drapes, doorways, bedspreads–nothing is sacred. He is just making sure no intruding males get the mistaken notion that they can move in on his turf. The best thing to do is to interrupt this behavior as soon as you see your dog do it. Small dogs can be more difficult to break of this habit than the larger breeds. Undoubtedly, a good part of the reason is that they can get into the habit of doing this before their behavior is noticed. Neutered males are far less likely to mark than their sexually entire brothers.

## Chewing

All dogs chew, and they do so for a whole lot of reasons. To begin with, dogs do everything with their mouths that we do with our hands. We humans, who should know better, do some terribly destructive things to relieve tension and escape from anxiety or frustration. Smoking cigarettes or compulsive eating are not exactly healthy measures, yet we continue to do them.

Dogs also chew to relieve anxiety and stress. Dogs that aren't given sufficient exercise use up some of that energy by chewing. Puppies experiment by chewing; they test everything they come across to see what it is, what it tastes like, and what it's made of. They chew to relieve the pressure of those tiny new teeth trying to burst their way through the gums.

Most dogs will chew anything that comes across their paths, even the couch.

There are a lot of reasons puppies chew—some of the results are acceptable in human society, some of them are not. Chewing is good when it is done on a bone or a safe chew toy, but bad when it takes place on the corner of your new coffee table or oriental rug.

Giving your dog things to occupy his time and taking the dog with you when you run errands or take short trips helps to keep his canine mind interested and active. There are very few dogs that are willing to sit around day after day with absolutely nothing to do that won't eventually pick up something to relieve that boredom.

If you know your dog is inclined to chew and you leave him in the living room when you go to the movies, expect him to have obliged your negligence. If, on the other hand, he is tucked safely away in his crate or his own small area with something to occupy his jaws, you can come home without fear that the entire encyclopedia set has been digested.

## Jumping Up

As much as most of us like dogs and really don't mind them jumping up on us for joy some of the time, there are other occasions when it is not appropriate for them to do so. The problem is that dogs don't understand that it is okay to jump up on you when you are wearing jeans but not okay when you are all dolled up and waiting for your date to arrive or you are on your way to the church social. Also, some people are terrified of dogs, and the last thing in the world they want is to have a dog leaping all over them. For all of these reasons and more, dogs must be taught not to jump up on anyone—ever—not even when they are puppies.

If your dog comes bounding up to greet you and plants his feet on you for a love pat, push those paws down

Help your dog understand that eating food off of the counter is unacceptable.

and command, "Off!" Just as soon as all four of the dog's feet are on the ground, praise him lavishly. Remember to use only the off command and no other. Don't say "Down" unless you actually want your dog to lie down. Don't try saying "No" one time and "Scoot" the next. Success depends upon your dog associating the behavior with the word.

One of the problems you may face is that some people will ignore your wishes and say, "Oh, I don't mind, I have dogs of my own. I love them all." They are trying to be nice, but nevertheless, they are making your training job more difficult. You'll have to be direct about this situation and simply tell the person that you appreciate their kindness but that you are in the process of trying to teach the dog not to jump up on people. I'm sure they'll understand and respect your wishes.

The no-jumping-up rule has to apply to everyone in the family as well. It's difficult for a dog to determine who doesn't mind or when the behavior is acceptable, and because it's something that dogs like to do, the lesson will take forever to get across if everyone in the household doesn't cooperate.

## Digging

There's hardly a dog I know that doesn't like to dig. Most dogs do it outdoors, but I've known some that like nothing better than digging their way through a down comforter or sofa cushion. The urge to dig is just a dog being a dog, but destructiveness is something that has to be dealt with quickly and in no uncertain terms.

Give your dog a designated place in which to dig.

Outdoor digging is harmless unless it is in the middle of the lawn or in your newly planted flowerbed. When this is the case, you'll be glad that the no command was one of the first lessons you taught your dog. The dog that minds extremely well may be content to leave it at that. However, a lot of other dogs may simply move on to another part of the flowerbed or lawn and start digging again.

Giving your dog his own "sandbox" could be the answer. To get the dog digging in his own place the first time, bury a bone or special treat there. You may even have to help him find the buried treasure a time or two, but most dogs get the idea in a hurry and the problem may be solved.

However, some dogs are a little more determined than that. The only cure for the problem in this case may be keeping a watchful eye on the dog when you are together and when you can't be watching, keeping the dog away from the area you do not want excavated.

## Sexual Behavior

Male dogs, in some cases even those that have been sexually altered, may mount people's legs or even inanimate objects. It can originate as a sexual urge or as an attempt to dominate. Bitches also display similar behavior when they are in season or asserting dominance. At any rate, it must be discouraged at the dog's first attempts to do so. Owners will often think it's cute when a puppy does it, but live to regret not curbing the dog's desire to mount when it becomes a frequent embarrassment or even a danger to the elderly or small children. Stopping this behavior immediately is the best way to avoid problems later on.

Although it is unacceptable behavior, dogs jump up as a way of greeting people.

### Cause and Effect

There are seldom hard and fast answers to solving behavior problems for all dogs. Understanding the cause of the problem is the first step in correcting it. Then, too, it is important for the trainer to understand how important it is to keep bad habits from being established in the first place. If the bad habit cycle has already started, there is no substitute for the positive reinforcement of good behavior.

# Family Fun

Your dog has become a valued member of the family. The hours that you spent teaching your canine companion how to behave have paid off. He is now welcomed at many of the places you go and can do almost anything with you. This means that there is a world of fun out there for you to experience, including vacations for the whole family, organized fun activities like agility and flyball, and plenty of just-plain-fun things to do as well.

## Exercise

There's a bonus to all the care and attention that you give your dog. He returns the favor by requiring exercise, which is something he needs to keep him from getting bored and to keep him in shape.

Exercise keeps your dog physically fit and mentally stimulated.

*These playmates keep each other company.*

However, it is also something that will do nothing but improve your own health and state of mind. You don't have to become a tri-athlete to give your dog the exercise he needs. Just walking at an invigorating pace is good for both you and your pet.

A dog's energy level isn't ignored as easily as ours is. It will be used up in some way, and if you would prefer your dog to use it by excavating a hole through the wall-to-wall carpeting or taking down the drapery, the choice is yours. Most owners would prefer to have their dogs use up their energy by taking a good brisk walk, playing catch, or bringing back a Frisbee™.

Puppies usually get all of the exercise they need on their own, especially if they have a playmate. However, there are very few adult dogs that get the exercise they need without opportunity and encouragement. As maturity and old age set in, you'll find dogs become less inclined to be self-starters when it comes to exercise. But interestingly, the laziest dog in town is more than willing to forego his afternoon snooze if his owner extends an invitation to go somewhere–anywhere!

Whenever you start on a new form of exercise with your dog, do so gradually and increase the duration of the workout very slowly. Do not start jogging with a young dog–wait at

### Did You Know?

Puppies play hard with their littermates, but you will note that after brief bouts of high-level activity, they all settle down for a good long nap. Puppies need exercise, but they should be given ample time to rest. Don't expect a baby pup to take a ten-mile hike. The smart pup will plunk his little rear down and refuse to budge, and you will have to tote the little fellow all the way back home. Never push a puppy beyond his limits, and wait until he matures before planning heavy exercise sessions.

## Swimming

Most dogs love to swim, and there couldn't be any better exercise for them. Any place that is safe for a child to swim will be safe for your dog as well. Some dogs love the water so much they can be too adventurous for their own good. Make sure you don't send your pal into a dangerous situation. Never allow your dog to be around a pool until you are sure that the dog can swim well and that he knows how and where to get out of the pool. Many dogs have drowned in pools while their owners were away because they were never taught to find the pool stairs.

least until the dog is 18 months of age. By then, the dog's bones and muscles have formed and strengthened to the point where there will be no permanent damage.

Be careful about exercising in hot weather. Confine exercise periods to the early morning hours before temperatures rise or until temperatures drop down in the evening.

If you own a senior dog, it doesn't mean he should stop exercising. The older fellow will still enjoy taking those walks with you every day. Maybe he won't be thrilled about heading outdoors on cold or blustery days, but a sweater or doggie coat will protect him. When the weather is nice, there is absolutely no reason why the two of you can't be out taking a leisurely walk around the block or down to the park. Use discretion when throwing balls and playing fetch, even though the dog might think he is still capable of doing the 100-yard dash. Be kind and be careful when it comes to exercising your senior dog, and he'll be with you for a much longer time.

Also, eating properly and maintaining a sensible exercise program will keep the whole family (both human and canine) happier and healthier.

Swimming is a fun and safe form of exercise for most dogs.

A nutritious diet and sensible exercise program will keep your dog in tip-top shape.

Make your family vacation as pet friendly as possible.

## Family Vacations

Now that your dog is well trained, why not have him share the fun you will all be having on that summer vacation? The streets of a big city or Aunt Tilly's small apartment may not be the best place take your dog, but there are all kinds of vacation plans you can make that will easily accommodate the whole family, including your canine pal.

Again, it's simply a matter of planning ahead and knowing what destinations will offer the most pleasure and convenience for all of you. The following are simply some suggestions that may appeal to you or inspire you to come up with an idea that would be even more suitable for you and your family.

Lakeside cottages and cabins in the mountains provide a degree of privacy, yet plenty of opportunity for family fun and social events in nearby towns. Your dog will get as big a kick out of boating and swimming as the rest of the family, and although dogs aren't the most proficient fishermen in the world, they are among the most enthusiastic.

A hiking or camping trip provides the whole family with lots of fun and adventure, to say nothing of the excellent exercise in the great outdoors. It should go without saying that dog owners should be particularly aware of camp and trail rules and obey them to the letter.

## Just for the Fun of It

Some people think that dogs aren't capable of having a sense of humor, but I disagree. I've had too many dogs in my life that were considered stand-up comedians among their peers. They did silly things that always elicited laughter from everyone in the family, and they did so with tails wagging and a sparkle in their eyes.

Other dogs I've owned approached life a bit more seriously, but that doesn't mean they were devoid of personality or that they didn't enjoy joining in on the fun. Because there are so many fun activities that dogs are capable of participating in with their owners, it would take an entire book just to list and explain them. Some owners find their dogs are so good at certain games and activities that they set about pursuing slightly more formal outlets of exercise. Again, the sky's the limit. There are countless activities that provide the exercise that dogs need, as well as being limitless fun for both owner and dog.

*Training sessions should be varied and enjoyable.*

## Obedience

If you and your dog enjoy training exercises, you may want to start training for obedience titles. Some dogs take to formal obedience work like the proverbial duck takes to water. Mixed or purebred, there are dogs that seem to love the thrill of performing, and the many levels of obedience work give them the opportunity to show off their skills. The details about how to get involved in obedience trials and what they entail are covered in the chapter on obedience training.

In order to succeed in obedience, however, the owner has to feel enthusiastic about it. If you look at the training required for these trials as drudgery, it will take the fun out of it, and this attitude can transfer to the dog. Find out more about obedience competition and see if it is for you.

*An enthusiastic attitude toward training will help motivate your dog.*

### Flyball Titles

Titles can be earned, including: Flyball Dog (FD), Flyball Dog Excellent (FDX), and Flyball Dog Champion (FDCh.). Information regarding rules, training, and places where the events are held can be obtained directly from the North American Flyball Association, Inc.

*Most dogs enjoy mastering the obstacles in agility competitions.*

## Flyball

Flyball is undoubtedly one of the most exciting activities in which you and your dog can participate. In this event, the dogs are organized into four teams. Each team races on a relay system. At the signal, each dog must clear four hurdles, release a ball from the fly ball box, catch it in the air, and return with the ball to the starting point so that the next teammate can start. The team is racing against the clock, and the speed and excitement usually encourage the very enthusiastic ringside crowd.

## Agility

Agility competition is basically an obstacle course for dogs. Everyone involved, including the spectators, appears to be having the time of their lives, and the sport has become tremendously popular at dog shows and exhibitions from coast to coast. There are tunnels, catwalks, seesaws, and numerous other obstacles that the canine contestants have to master off leash while they are being timed. It takes teamwork because the handler has to act as navigator.

Although the dogs do all the maneuvering, it is the handler who directs the dog, because the sequence of the individual obstacles is different at every event. Both the American Kennel Club and the US Dog Agility Association can provide additional information, as well as names and addresses of the organizations sponsoring events nearest to your home.

## Frisbee™

Catching a Frisbee™ may not be every dog's "game du jour," but the dogs that love it, love it–catching that plastic disc while it flies through the air becomes an obsession with them. For those addicted canines, there are local, regional, and national Frisbee™ competitions.

## Freestyle

Freestyle is something new for the canine athlete that might also be somewhat musically inclined. The sport combines obedience, dance, and calisthenics. Many of the basic obedience exercises are used, but in Freestyle, the movements are choreographed into a routine that is set to music. There are two main approaches to Freestyle: The Canine Freestyle Federation (CFF) emphasizes the dogs' movements; the Musical Canine Sports International (MCSI) has a somewhat more colorful approach to the event, with consideration given to the handlers' movements and costuming. Enthusiasm, the degree of difficulty in the movements displayed, and appropriateness of music and its interpretation are additional scoring factors. Detailed information can be obtained directly from the Canine Freestyle Federation.

## Dogs that Serve

Although work as a therapy dog isn't considered a sport, it certainly brings great joy to the children and adults who benefit from the visits. Dogs that have calm demeanors and good manners are best suited to make visits to hospitals, long-term care facilities, and orphanages. Children and the elderly especially seem to light up when these dogs visit them, and it is amazing how sweet and gentle the therapy dogs can be.

### Did You Know?

Frisbee™ competitions offer cash prizes ranging for hundreds to thousands of dollars. There are even international Frisbee™ teams that meet annually for the World Cup!

Leading pet shops usually carry information on these competitions. Both the Friskies Canine Frisbee™ Championships and the Alpo Frisbee™ Contest also provide information on their competitions.

**Part 2**

Freestyle gives your dog the chance to show off his dance moves.

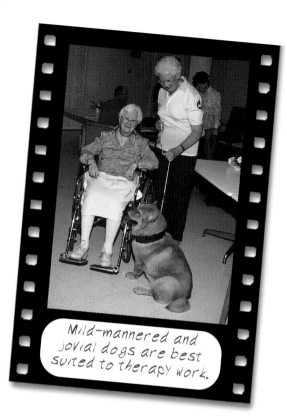

Mild-mannered and jovial dogs are best suited to therapy work.

It does take some training, because the dogs will be faced with situations they normally wouldn't be confronted with at home. The effort involved for dog and owner is more than rewarded in the sunshine it brings into peoples lives. Therapy Dogs International and the Delta Society can both provide additional information.

# On the Road with Rover

Travel is a part of everyday life. Whether you travel across town, across the state, or across the country, the decision will have to be made about what to do with your canine pal.

I have never owned a dog that hasn't hurled himself toward the door upon the first rattle of my car keys, and that includes the dogs that spent the first few months of traveling so carsick, I was certain they would never get past it.

I have friends who have occupations that keep them in their automobiles as many as five days a week and often for many hours at a stretch. They have helped to relieve the boredom by taking their dogs along

*Most dogs look forward to road trips with their owners.*

Take every precaution to ensure your dog's safety while traveling.

Love and care are all a dog really needs to be happy.

with them on their trips, and they enjoy the company immensely. Dogs can be wonderful travel companions without saying a word. They are never back seat drivers, nor do they complain if you choose to sing at the top of your lungs–off-key.

Whether you travel down the street or take a long journey, there are certain things that must be considered before you embark. The longer you plan to be gone, the more preparation it will take. If you plan to fly, there are a number of legal requirements that must be attended, in addition to purchasing the proper travel crate and having your dog's necessary inoculations up to date.

If you decide that your dog should not travel with you and there is no one at home for him to stay with, other arrangements have to be made for his care. You may decide to have a friend take care of him, or you may choose to keep him in a boarding kennel or to hire a pet sitter to come to your home.

These are all issues that will have to be addressed at some time during the years you and your dog will spend together. There is no time like the present to begin thinking about how you will handle travel when the time does come.

## By Land

If you will be hitting the highway, you should think about protection for both your dog and your car. Puppies and adult dogs love the scent of leather seats, and if it smells good, there is no doubt in a dog's mind that it must taste good, too. What better way for your dog to pass the time while you are arguing with the garage mechanic or filling up the gas tank? Chewing up the leather seats or taking the stuffing out from under the cloth upholstery is great fun–for your dog! Even if you are driving a car that is destined for the junkyard, understand that only so much upholstery can be removed until you are sitting on the seat springs–and upholstery is not the best thing in the world for your dog's digestive system. If you must leave your dog alone in the car for a short period of time, make sure he has a bone or toy to keep him occupied. Throwing an old sheet or blanket over the backseat can also deter you dog from chewing, as well as help make cleaning up after him easier.

## Did You Know?

If you plan to stay with friends while you travel, the crate will really come in handy, especially if your hosts do not have other dogs in the house. Even if the household has one or more dogs of their own, they may not be entirely thrilled at the arrival of your pal. The hosts' dog and your dog will not always be able to work it all out between themselves. A crate will offer your pet a place of safety and refuge in a strange environment.

There are also dangers to having your dog riding unrestrained in the car. Sudden stops could throw him against the front window or dashboard and injure him seriously. Any dog can become excited and interfere with your driving at a critical moment. For these and many other reasons, there is nothing safer for your car or for your dog than traveling in a crate or restrained by a doggy seat belt.

Many of the hotels and motels that accept pets expect you to confine your dog while he is in your room. Again, the crate that he is accustomed to staying in is the best bet. If your dog requires a crate that is too big for your car, carry along a collapsible-type crate that you can stow in your trunk, and ask your pet supply store about a doggy seat belt. Beyond a shadow of a doubt, seat belts have been proven to be lifesavers and can provide the same measure of safety for your dog.

Check to see if your accommodations are pet friendly before traveling.

## Safety on the Road

Two of the most important factors to consider before embarking on a trip of any length are the temperature and the length of time required for the stops you will be making. Summer outdoor temperatures won't matter much if you and you dog are traveling in an air-conditioned car or van—if you don't plan to stop. If you plan to stop at all in hot weather, think ahead about whether or not you will be able to take your dog indoors with you. Most restaurants and other public buildings in the United States do not permit dogs. The only place for your dog will then be locked in the car—a dangerous and often deadly place for any dog, especially in warm weather.

If you like to drive with your windows down, safely securing your dog will prevent him from hanging his head out the window–something all dogs seem to enjoy doing. Flying sticks, stones, and other debris can seriously damage your dog's eyes, so take measures to keep your dog's head in the car.

Give your dog some outside time before hitting the road.

The safest rule to follow is never to leave your pet in a vehicle unattended. Leaving the windows down is also not an option. No matter how well you have trained your dog, good sense is going to make him want to get out in a hurry if it gets too hot inside the car. This could cost the dog his life.

Open car windows give would-be thieves easy access to your dog. Dog theft has escalated alarmingly in the past few years and someone looking for an easy "reward" just may be lurking by.

If its a very hot day and you know will have to make stops along the way–leave your dog home in a cool room or shaded run.

### Identification

Positive identification of your dog is most important during the time you are traveling. An accident may occur, throwing your dog out of the car, or he could wander off when you make a stop. Once loose in a strange area, dogs are inclined to panic and run further and further away from where they should be. Your dog should wear dog tags indicating the person to contact. Also, be sure that there will be someone at that contact point to receive the message that your dog has been found. Keep these ID tags on your dog at all times.

## Inoculations

If you are planning to drive across the border to Canada or Mexico, your dog will be required to possess health certificates validated by your veterinarian and to have an up-to-date vaccination against rabies. Most states throughout the US will also require rabies inoculations. Be sure your dog is wearing the tag your veterinarian will issue when he is vaccinated. Depending upon your destination, he will also be able to advise you on any special precautions that you might have to take. For example, certain sections of the country put your dog at risk for tick-borne Lyme disease and heartworm.

## Packing Up

Planning ahead for a road trip can make even the longest journey completely enjoyable. After you have made out the list of your personal needs, do the same for your dog.

Changing food suddenly can cause diarrhea, hardly what you want during a trip. Bring enough food and water to last the length of the trip, as well as food and water dishes. A brush, comb, and dry bath product will keep your pooch clean and smelling nice. Remember that your dog will be in a closed car with you for hours on end, so this is important.

### Did You Know?

Perhaps 80-degree weather doesn't seem unreasonable to you, but on a sunny day, in a closed car, that temperature can soar up to well over 100 degrees in a few minutes. In less than 30 minutes, the temperature could be heading toward 125 degrees. No dog could sustain these temperatures without suffering irreparable brain damage.

**Part 2**

Your pet should be up to date with his vaccinations prior to traveling.

Part 2

Planning ahead can make even a long trip enjoyable.

## Microchips

An even better and more permanent method of identification available now is the microchip—a tiny computer chip that is implanted under the dog's skin at the base of the dog's neck. The chip is read by a scanner, and most local veterinarians carry and implant the chips. Humane societies throughout the country are equipped with these scanners, and more and more organizations and veterinary hospitals are becoming similarly equipped. The number on the chip can be registered with organizations such as the American Kennel Club's Home Again microchip program or the International American Veterinary Identification Systems, Inc.(AVID). The latter is an international identification organization with offices and contact numbers throughout the world.

A solid or collapsible crate like the Fold-Away Pet Carrier™ can solve many problems as you travel. For those stops that you'll have to make, you'll need a good long leash and sturdy collar with ID tags attached. A list of parks and rest stops along the way can make life easier, and be sure to bring a poop scooper and a good supply of plastic grocery bags for cleanups. Your dog's favorite toys will help him to pass the long travel hours or the times you are off sightseeing. Long-lasting bones available at pet shops are ideal to provide hours of chewing fun.

## By Air

Traveling by air takes a good deal more advance preparation than traveling by car. If your dog is small enough to fit under the seat in front of you, this will eliminate a lot of the technicalities. If this is the case, you must reserve space for your dog ahead of time as you make your reservation, because only a limited number of animals may be carried on board

## Hotels and Motels

Not all hotels and motels accept dogs. The days of traveling until you are totally exhausted and checking into the first hotel or motel you see are a thing of the past when your canine pal is accompanying you. There are some wonderful resources you can refer to that will help to avoid accommodation problems. It is wise to contact places you plan to visit well before you leave for your trip.

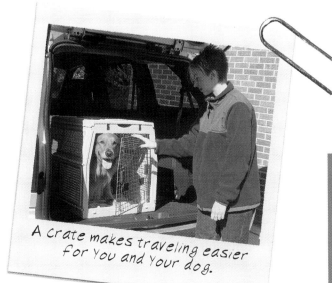

A crate makes traveling easier for you and your dog.

per flight. Your dog will have to be in a safe and secure carrier that will fit under the seat. There are no exceptions to this rule, and there is an additional charge for bringing your dog aboard a plane.

If your dog will not fit under the seat in front of you, he must fly as excess baggage in the cargo hold of the plane at a cost determined by the airline. Air travel for dogs is no longer a unique situation. Each day, airlines accommodate hundreds of dogs accompanying their owners back and forth across the country. The Department of Agriculture estimates that approximately 600,000 animals a year travel by air, and a good percentage of that number is made up of dogs and cats. The Air Transport Association reports that 99 percent of all animals shipped in the US reach their destination without incident.

There are numerous safety measures that you can take to increase the odds of a safe trip for your dog. Begin by calling the airlines to check out their policies regarding shipping dogs, and select the airline that offers the greatest safety assurances.

Most airlines will only accept a predetermined number of dogs per flight in the cargo hold, so you must make

### Did You Know?

If your dog will be traveling in the cargo area of the plane, it should be understood that while this area is pressurized, there is no air-conditioning or heat control. Thus, federal regulations and embargoes placed by the airlines themselves forbid any animal to be shipped by air if the ground temperature at either end of the flight is above 85 degrees or below 45 degrees.

Plan ahead to ensure that you and your pet have a comfortable and safe trip.

Most airlines will require a health certificate signed by your vet.

a reservation in advance. This will also signal to the airline that they will be unable to accept shipments at that time that contain dry ice or other substances that might harm a live animal. Your travel agent will able to do this for you when making your own reservation. However, reconfirm (and then reconfirm again) before flight time.

Always schedule direct, nonstop flights. Changing planes and stopovers are just some of the ways you increase the risk of something going wrong. I strongly recommend overnight and very early morning flights. They are normally the least crowded and temperatures are more moderate at that time, especially during the summer months.

Most states require a health certificate signed by a veterinarian and nearly all airlines will require one whether your destination does or not. The crate you ship your dog in must be approved by the airline. Most pet supply stores sell crates that are guaranteed to be airline approved. It must be sturdy enough and large enough for your dog to stand up and turn around in. Don't think that bigger is better, however. Just enough room protects your dog from being jostled about.

Federal law requires absorbent bedding on the bottom of the crate. You must also supply food and water in dishes that are attached to the inside of the crates wire door. Tape a small bag of food to the top of the crate, along with food and water instructions for the next 24 hours in case of delays. You are not allowed to put a lock on the crate door; however, you can offer double security with bungee cords or tape.

A "Live Animal" sticker must be placed on the crate. Airlines will have these stickers available at your point of departure. Tape a sign to the crate that provides full information, including phone numbers and addresses of contact persons at your point of departure and your destination.

Regardless of how careful everyone might be, accidents do happen and a dog may manage to escape from his crate. Make sure your dog has ID tags attached to his collar. Include a telephone number at which someone can be reached 24 hours a day on the tag.

Your dog's tags should include his name and a contact number.

Most airlines want you to get to the airport a minimum of an hour and a half before flight time. When you do arrive, go directly to the passenger check-in counter. Make sure the dog is fully checked in, but insist that you stay where you can see the dog until it is time to transport the crate to the loading area. When you get on board, have the attendant check to make sure the dog actually is on board.

Leave your dog in the crate when you reach your destination until you can get to a place that is less frantic and a bit safer than the airline terminal. Have a good sturdy leash with you in your carry-on bag and snap the leash on your dog while he is still in the crate. This ensures that he will not be able to get away from you.

## Staying Behind

There are times when it just isn't practical to take your dog along with you. A friend might step in and help for a day or two, but you may prefer a good boarding kennel or a pet sitter to take good care of your pal while you're gone. Your vet or pet supply store can often make local recommendations.

### Boarding Kennels

Even with recommendations, no kennel is adequate for your dog unless it meets with your approval. When several kennels sound interesting, drop by during business hours and ask

**Part 2**

If you have to leave your dog behind, make sure he will be well taken care of.

Before leaving your dog in a kennel, make sure it is clean and well run.

if you can have a tour. There are several things you should investigate, beginning with sanitation. If the facility appears dirty and unkempt, go elsewhere.

Many kennels provide what they call play time. They will allow your dog time in a large paddock or run where someone can toss him a ball or a Frisbee™. They may charge a few dollars per day more for this service, but it can mean a big difference in your pal's stay.

Check to see what inoculations and health precautions boarders are required to have when they check in. Every reputable kennel will demand proof of current rabies inoculations and protection against kennel cough. Also, ask if incoming dogs are screened for fleas, ticks, and other parasites. If there are no requirements regarding health safeguards, I would strongly suggest looking for another kennel.

When you check your dog in, leave your veterinarian's name, address, and phone number with the kennel in case of an emergency, and leave a contact number where you can be reached while you're gone. Bring your dog's blanket and favorite toys. If the kennel does not feed your dog's preferred brand of dog food, bring enough from home to last for the duration of your absence.

## Pet Sitters

There are people who do not feel comfortable sending their pals to a boarding kennel. If this is the case, think about hiring a pet sitter. This is someone who will come to your home at regular intervals during the day to feed your dog, provide time for him to exercise, and let him out to take care of those calls of nature. Your veterinarian or pet shop may be able to recommend someone, or there are national organizations dedicated to making recommendations for qualified pet sitters.

*Hiring a pet sitter is an option if you are unable to travel with your dog.*

It is best to hire a professional pet sitter for many reasons. Most provide credentials and written agreements as to what they will do and for what they agree to be responsible. A professional is usually bonded and insured. This is very important, because anyone can advertise as a professional. You don't want to come home to find your dog sitting in a house that has been stripped of all your valuables. If you are unable to get a local recommendation or if the kennels or pet sitters in your area do not meet your needs, there are organizations that can assist you.

Part 2

# Part Three

# Keeping Your Dog Healthy

by Sara Thorton, DVM

# A Balanced Diet

A balanced diet is a key ingredient for proper canine health. Part of your dog's training should be to eat what you decide he should eat, not the other way around. With dogs, just like with children, dessert is more appealing than vegetables. Treats may be offered in moderation. A good idea would be to save treats for training and not to offer them frequently.

When adopting an adult dog, retraining the dog's food preferences may be necessary; a healthy dog will not starve himself to death. Offer small meals of the desired diet. Leave the food bowl down for 20 minutes, then pick up any leftovers. Do not offer any more food (including treats) until the next mealtime. A small amount of broth may be added to entice

A balanced diet is the key ingredient for sound health.

Choose a diet that best suits your dog's age and lifestyle.

Consult your vet as to which diet is right for your puppy.

the finicky canine, but don't worry if your dog skips meals for a day or two. Healthy dogs can go a few days without eating without long-term side effects.

There are basically three categories of generally available dog foods on the market: premium, commercial, and generic. As a rule of thumb, you get what you pay for when it comes to dog food.

1. Premium Diets: Premium diets, available in specialty shops and from your veterinarian, are more expensive, but they tend to be better digested and more consistent in quality. Often, the actual price of daily feeding is not considerably more than other diets, due to the concentration of calories per cup. In other words, a cup of premium diet may contain 400 calories, while another diet may only have 200 calories; you have to feed your dog twice as much to get the same number of calories.

2. Commercial Diets: Commercial diets are broadly available in supermarkets and pet stores. Most are national name brands that offer adequate to good nutrition for your canine.

3. Generic Diets: Generic or very low-cost budget brands usually will be poorly digested by your dog. Used regularly, they may lead to forms of malnutrition that may not be easily recognized by the pet owner. Veterinarians often diagnose gastrointestinal distress and skin problems associated with poor nutrition. It is better and more economical to feed a higher quality diet than to add a regimen of supplements.

## Formulas for Life Stages

Most diets are divided into different life stages. Dogs should be fed what is appropriate for both their ages

Part 3

## Dog Foods

Packaged dog foods generally come in three basic forms: dry kibble, canned, and semi-moist. Dry is the most economical to feed over the long run. Quality dry foods contain all the nutrients a healthy dog needs. Dry kibble also aids in preventing tartar buildup on the teeth by the abrasion when chewing. Canned food is highly palatable, but the drawback is the added expense to daily feeding. Many owners mix a small amount of canned food with dry to tempt a finicky eater. Semi-moist foods tend to be palatable, but more expensive to feed, plus they contain many additives.

An active dog will need a dog food that meets his physical needs.

Part 3

and their lifestyles. Your veterinarian may help you decide what is best. Some puppy foods are now available in regular and large-breed formulas (a large-breed dog is one that matures at 65 pounds or heavier). These are designed to regulate growth and to reduce the incidence of growth-related disorders.

Adult formulas vary widely. Better brands provide balanced nutrition for the average pet. High-protein diets are rarely indicated for pets; very few dogs have the metabolism or level of activity to handle these diets. Excess protein is hard on the kidneys.

Senior diets vary quite a bit. Some senior diets simply reduce fat and calories to accommodate for decreased activity. Active older dogs may do better on adult maintenance diets. Better senior diets reduce salt and adjust protein levels so that they are easier on the older dogs' metabolism.

In households with more than one dog, it may be necessary to separate the dogs at mealtime to ensure that each dog eats his appropriate diet. This will stop the gluttonous pet from deciding to take over the more timid pet's food. In addition, separation will guarantee that each pet will get the diet it needs. An easy way to separate them is to feed the dogs in different rooms or to provide the meal in their own crates.

A healthy diet should include the essential vitamins and minerals.

Some pet owners opt to feed their dogs homemade diets.

## Sorting Out the Facts

Natural diets have become very popular recently. However, the word "natural" on the label does not necessarily mean better nutrition. Preservatives do prevent dangerous degradation of foodstuffs. The quality of the natural food lines varies greatly and may be difficult for a pet owner to sort out.

A great deal is made over the protein source of dog foods. There is no magic in one source compared to another. Certainly, if a dog does not tolerate beef well, a chicken or lamb diet may be prudent. The important key to the protein source is how much, as well as how digestible, the diet is. Your veterinarian is a good source of advice for what is best for your dog.

Another current fad is to feed adult food to large-breed puppies in a misguided attempt to avoid orthopedic problems during growth. In reality, such a large amount must be fed to meet the necessary calorie requirements that the calcium content is much greater than recommended, which can cause bone disorders.

Owners certainly may prepare homemade diets for their pets. Contrary to popular myth, dogs are not true carnivores. Their dietary needs are probably closer to human diets. Well-meaning pet owners who feed their canines chicken breasts alone are not doing their beloved dogs any favors. There are numerous recipes available for homemade diets, usually containing about one-third meat protein, one-third carbohydrates (such as potato), and one-third vegetables. Most require a vitamin/mineral supplement to be added to the diet.

## Recipe for a Balanced Home-Cooked Meal

- 1 cup cooked rice or potato
- 1/4 pound cooked ground hamburger or lamb
- 1 Tbsp corn oil
- 1 cup corn, string beans or carrots
- 2 tsp. bone meal
- Vitamin/ mineral supplement

Mix all ingredients together. For an approximate feeding guide, feed one-half pound of this diet per 12 pounds of dog per day. So, a 24-pound dog would be fed one pound of this diet.

A current fad among some dog owners, especially certain breeders, is a raw food diet. Raw meat may expose your pets, as well as the people in your household, to parasites and bacteria such as salmonella and E. coli. The logic behind the raw food diet is that the raw foodstuffs are healthier and more natural. As breeds of dog have evolved, so have the ability of the dogs to digest. Certainly, a domestic Poodle cannot be expected to eat like a wild canid species would.

A modern means of disease control is the use of prescription diets to manage illness. These diets must be prescribed by a veterinarian and are designed for management of specific disease processes. Diabetes, kidney, liver, heart, gastrointestinal, and bladder diseases are some problems that special diets can aid in treating. Even dogs that undergo chemotherapy for some types of cancer may

A well-balanced and nutritious diet is the foundation of good health.

**Part 3**

## Allergies

Food allergies are becoming more commonly diagnosed in pets. Some dogs may not be able to tolerate dairy products and may get diarrhea whenever you slip them a bit of cheese or milk. It may be difficult to determine what the dog is allergic to. Blood tests are available to determine the offending foodstuff, but the traditional way is still the best way—the elimination diet. Change the dog's diet completely to ingredients he has never been exposed to. For example, if the dog has been on a number of commercial diets in the past, it may be necessary to utilize duck as a protein source and oats as the grain. Restriction to this diet takes two to eight weeks to see if symptoms of food allergy are relieved (rash and/or gastrointestinal distress). If symptoms improve, the dog may be challenged with one ingredient at a time to determine the food causing the allergy. The owner may start with beef, adding a small amount daily for two weeks to determine if there is a return of symptoms. Then, following beef, chicken may be added, and so on. With a diet trial, any cheating makes it null and void; this includes flavored vitamins or medication.

Maintaining a healthy lifestyle begins with the proper diet.

be aided by a prescribed diet designed for this special purpose. In order for these diets to be effective, most must be fed exclusively. Cheating does not help the dog.

### Supplements

Supplementation with vitamins and minerals is generally not necessary when feeding a quality, balanced diet, provided your pet is eating the food. Most premium diet manufacturers recommend against supplementation, because it may throw off an otherwise balanced diet. Minerals should be carefully managed. Unfortunately, quite a few breeders of large and giant dogs will recommend supplementing a diet with calcium to build bones. However, research has proven that this practice does more harm than good, and excess supplements in the diet can actually cause bone deformities leading to lameness.

When should dogs be given supplements? Occasionally, there are situations when supplements should be used. If your dog is a poor eater or undernourished from being fed poor-quality dog food, then a supplement can be added to the diet. If the dog is recovering from an illness, pregnant, or nursing puppies, then your veterinarian may recommend giving a supplement. Senior dogs also require vitamins and minerals, but you can get around giving supplements by feeding older dogs a high-quality senior diet, which contains the necessary supplements already.

## Nutritional Problems

Salt content in dog food is often considerably high. Dogs like salt, much as we enjoy salty potato chips. Dogs eat the salty chow, so their owners buy more. Dogs do develop high blood pressure and heart disease and require restricted sodium diets. Frequently, it is difficult to convince a dog to enjoy his change to a low-salt diet. Adding garlic or perhaps no-sodium chicken broth helps smooth the transition to the healthier diet.

Probably the most frequent nutritional problem seen by veterinarians is obesity, which is usually caused by feeding your dog too much. Overfeeding promotes diabetes and heart disease, as well as joint problems. Feeding a dog once daily does not mean he is consuming fewer calories. It is better to feed a small amount twice daily and reduce the number of calories per day. Keep in mind that treats count as well. Many overweight dogs may snack on low-calorie treats such as plain popcorn, carrots, or rice cakes to reduce calories in the diet. Your veterinarian may

Feed your dog a diet that is both low in salt and fat.

**Part 3**

### Beware of Dog

Any change in a dog's diet should be performed gradually to avoid stomach or bowel upset. It is best to feed a consistent diet as opposed to changing foods frequently. Maintaining consistency makes it easier to manage your pet's health, especially when it comes to your dog's weight, as different brands may provide drastically different numbers of calories.

*Good food and daily exercise will increase the longevity of your pet's life.*

need to rule out thyroid or adrenal gland disease in a dog that has difficulty losing weight. If all checks out normally, reduced food and increased exercise must be pursued. An owner should be able to easily feel his dog's ribs; if you run your hands down his sides and cannot feel the ribs, he is probably overweight.

## Giving Treats and Snacks

Treats and snacks should be kept to a minimum. Utilizing them in training is better than giving them unearned. Insist that your dog sits or lies down before rewarding him with a favorite snack. This enforces the fact that you are in control of the food—and, thus, the pet.

Chewing can be very beneficial for both puppies and older dogs. Chewing on chew toys like Nylabones® will help scrape away tartar, which in turn will help keep your dog's teeth clean and breath fresh. For some dogs, chewing gives them great pleasure and will keep them from getting bored. There are many chewy treats on the

*It's best to give your dog treats during training as rewards.*

### Healthy Treats

Most commercial dog treats are full of salt and calories. Table food may be too spicy or full of fat. Moderation is the key with these foodstuffs. If your dog has a weight problem, these items must be very limited. If your dog has a disease such as diabetes or kidney or heart failure, consult your veterinarian before giving any treats.

market, but you must be careful only to give your pet safe objects to chew on.

Bones should never be given to dogs. Forget the argument that dogs eat bones naturally. Chicken bones splinter and can lacerate the gastrointestinal lining or can become lodged in the throat or the mouth. Ham and steak bones also become lodged in the mouth or along the alimentary tract, causing life-threatening obstructions. Even the very large bones on the market can break teeth and damage dental enamel. There are plenty of man-made nylon or processed food bones like Nylabones® available in pet stores that will supply a dog with hours of oral bliss. Nylabones® are sold in a variety of flavors and sizes, many of which are 100-percent digestible.

Chewing helps remove tartar and keeps your dog's breath fresh.

Rawhides are a staple of most pet supply stores. Only buy high-quality rawhides that look clean and fresh. If the rawhide becomes dirty or moldy after your dog chews on it, throw it away. Do not allow your dog to continue chewing on filthy or spoiled pieces. While they can keep a dog busy for a long time–especially the compressed version– they may contribute to bowel problems, including constipation. Again, careful observation and management is vital to protect your dog's health. Do not leave your puppy alone with rawhide toys and make sure he does not swallow big pieces of it, because it can lead to intestinal blockage.

Give your dog safe, age-appropriate chew toys like Nylabones®.

Pig ears and chew hooves are popular treats that dogs love and, yes, they are truly made from the ears of pigs and animal hooves. Most dogs find both of these treats to be irresistible. Pig ears are high in both fat and protein, while chew hooves are composed of 100-percent protein. Because they are natural animal products, they are completely digestible (unlike rawhide). However, hooves can splinter like bones, so give these treats only under supervision. Pig ears and chew hooves may be natural, but they're still treats and not food, so they must be limited in the diet. Give these to your dog only in moderation and not every day.

Table food does contribute to obesity and can irritate the dog's gastrointestinal tract. Any scraps from the family dinner should be given in very limited portions. Spicy foods should be avoided completely, because your dog's stomach can be sensitive.

## Water

Fresh, clean water should be available at all times. Water is the most essential nutrient, and deprivation can lead to rapid death. Be especially vigilant during hot days in the summer, when your dog may be drinking more water than usual. Keep a close eye on your dog's water bowl to make sure it does not go dry during hot spells. Don't forget to carry water and a drinking container with you when you travel with your pet. If you're on a long trip, stop at regular intervals to let your pet drink and romp a bit before crating him again.

If you observe increased water consumption, promptly take your dog to the veterinarian, as diabetes, adrenal gland imbalance, or other diseases could be the cause. If your dog is drinking more than normal, limiting water availability is not an answer and can be dangerous.

Like humans, dogs are also susceptible to illness contracted from contaminated water, including giardia. If there is a water advisory in the area, your pet's water should be boiled before drinking, as well as all of your household water.

Water is an essential part of your dog's diet.

# Exercise for Fitness

Exercise is a primary component of every healthy dog's life plan. The amount of time an owner can devote to recreation with a dog should be a primary influence on what type of canine joins the family. All dogs need exercise. Walks to relieve your dog's bowels and bladder provide recreation, but for most dogs, this is not nearly enough.

Many breeds require much more than several daily walks. For example, herding breeds were developed to herd sheep or cattle all day long, which is a tremendous amount of activity. Sporting breeds were designed to work in the field retrieving or finding game. Expecting these dogs to become sedate couch potatoes is unrealistic.

Exercise is a good way for your dog to release excess energy.

Monitoring your puppy's exercise can help prevent injury.

Try to engage your dog in activities that he enjoys, such as swimming.

Not only are less active dogs more likely to develop health problems, but behavior problems may occur as well. A tired dog is a good dog. An underactive dog tends to be bored and may look to find things to do; boredom lends itself to problem behaviors such as digging holes, chewing, barking, and raiding the trash. Exercise relieves stress and releases energy in active breeds. With owner participation, exercise contributes to close bonding and fun. Dogs love to participate in everyday activities; more than a few have been trained to fetch the paper or a pair of slippers.

## Puppies and Exercise

For puppies, exercise builds bones and confidence. Games, walks, and even swimming develop their growing bodies' strength and endurance. Puppies may tire easily and should not be pushed beyond their limits. Several short periods of activity throughout the day are more valuable than one or two long sessions.

With some puppies, owners must use good judgment, as they will try to do more than they are capable of handling, such as a long retrieve or lengthy walk with a companion. They are babies and do not recognize their limitations. Responsible pet owners will observe their pups closely for signs of fatigue, including a decrease in enthusiasm, slowing of gait, or excessive panting.

## Adult Dogs and Exercise

Mature dogs thrive with active lives. Regular walks, swimming, and games such as fetch maintain mental and physical fitness. Dogs love to do what they were bred to do. Retrievers love to retrieve, pointers love to seek game, and herders love to herd. Family activities can be arranged around canine sports such as herding tests.

## Older Dogs and Exercise

Senior pets benefit from the stimulation that a regular exercise program provides. Although their eyesight and agility may preclude a rigorous game of fetch, most still enjoy a relaxing outing. Dogs with arthritis and heart disease benefit from regular light exercise. If your senior pal seems too uncomfortable for this, a veterinarian should be consulted.

On a more basic level, including the family dog in routine fitness activities such as jogging or biking is good for both the owner and the dog. A well-trained dog is a necessity in these sports. Owner and dog need to navigate safely along roads. Canine companions may also be trained to assist with everyday chores, such as carrying trash bags, firewood, or garden tools. This gives your dog a sense of purpose and therefore relieves stress.

## Exercise Precautions

With any pet, care should be taken outdoors during extreme weather. All dogs are subject to heatstroke during hot weather, because they are unable to sweat to release heat through their skin. Panting helps to cool the body temperature, but it is not always enough. Breeds with short faces, such as Bulldogs and Pugs, are particularly vulnerable to heatstroke.

In extremely cold weather, frigid air entering the lungs may cause irritation and damage. Slipping on ice can damage joints. Salt on sidewalks may irritate paws. Most important, inadequate shelter and/or prolonged exposure may cause frostbite or hypothermia. However, some breeds, such as Alaskan Malamutes or Siberian Huskies, do tolerate cold weather well.

Before attempting any exercise program for your pet, a thorough physical examination by a veterinarian is in order to discuss appropriate exercises and limitations. For example, small,

Be careful not to exercise your dog too heavily during extreme weather conditions.

Like humans, dogs need to build up their endurance levels.

**Beware for Dog**

Any exercise should be delayed until meals are well digested, which is about one hour. This will help avoid gastric upset and may help avoid bloat, a life-threatening condition.

short-legged dogs cannot be expected to run alongside bicycles. Brief walks are appropriate for short-faced breeds, including English Bulldogs and Pekingese. Dogs with joint disorders or heart disease cannot be expected to perform strenuously.

## Conditioning and Sports Injuries

After your pet gets a green light for exercise, conditioning is the next step. Dogs require aerobic conditioning to build endurance, as well as muscle conditioning to reduce injuries. Common sense should prevail; a dog that is not in shape should not attempt a five-mile run. The mind may be willing, but the body will suffer. Start your pet with reduced intensity workouts and short-duration activities, such as a half-mile to one-mile walk. Do this several times a week, gradually increasing the speed and distance.

Some dogs develop problems with soreness and fatigue, as well as increased vulnerability to injury when owners follow an exercise program on weekends only. Being inactive all week, then going all out on the weekend, is difficult for dogs as well as humans. Owners should be kind and keep this in mind.

Dogs are subject to sports injuries. Even a well-conditioned dog may experience a pulled muscle or worse, a torn ligament. If lameness persists beyond a day or two, your dog's veterinarian should be consulted. Another sort of injury common in dogs is broken teeth.

Part 3

Owners don't always consider when throwing a ball or other hard object that their canine may get a little too enthusiastic and bite down.

Paws may need extra protection for constant pounding on hard surfaces. Sport boots are manufactured for dogs to protect their foot pads. Also, solutions are available to toughen the pads.

## Turning Playtime into Competitive Sports

Most dogs love playtime. Catching a Frisbee™, a ball, or a stick, running alongside their favorite person, and even navigating an obstacle course of small jumps will keep your dog happy and healthy. These activities may be pursued for fun or may be elevated to a competitive sport. Most require little equipment, while a few need a substantial amount of extras.

Competitive Frisbee™ requires only a plastic disc, a healthy, agile dog, and an open field. Competitive obedience starts off with only a collar and a leash at the lower levels. At the higher levels, a dumbbell is added, then a set of jumps and, finally, scent articles. Agility may be performed simply using boards as planks to walk on or may be developed into an advanced sport using tunnels and seesaws. Weight pulling requires owners to provide an appropriate harness, but the weight that the dog pulls can be an old tire. Practice with weights has developed dogs that could pull over 5,000 pounds. Of course, most dogs cannot safely pull heavy weights, but can develop strength over a period of time.

All dogs are capable of learning to track. Dogs have excellent olfactory sense, and some, such as the

Most dogs, especially retrievers, like to play in the water.

The pleasure of training your dog is the greatest reward.

**Part 3**

*Whether you're training your dog for fun or competition, the benefits are enduring.*

Bloodhound, are exceptional at tracking. Tracking does not require a lot of fancy equipment, only your time and patience. Herding trials are available throughout the country to demonstrate both instinct and training in these breeds. Of course, there must be livestock available to participate.

For sporting breeds, hunting tests and field trials are popular competitions. These test both the instinct and training of the participating breeds. Lure coursing is available for owners of sighthounds like Whippets or Greyhounds. These tests evaluate the natural instinct in these breeds. Earthdog trials give the terriers a chance to strut their stuff, following rodent scent into tunnels. As compared to the above-mentioned sports, which attract many participants, Schutzhund training should only be attempted by the serious owner of working breeds. It involves tracking, obedience, and protection training, requiring a tremendous commitment of time and energy.

Whether you and your dog pursue a sport for fun and exercise or for the competition, the rewards can be outstanding. Planning activities with your dog may start early with puppy preschool, offered at many veterinary offices and some pet stores. Training and activities are a lifetime pursuit, with obedience classes, handling classes, and even trick classes available. The pleasure of training your dog is greater than any trophy you may win.

# The Well-Groomed Dog

## Nail Care

All pets need some form of grooming. Probably the most overlooked portion of regular grooming is nail care. While dogs that spend a good part of their day outdoors running on rough surfaces may wear down their nails naturally, indoor dogs do not have this advantage. Even when outside, your dog may spend most of his time on soft grass, and his nails are not being worn down. Therefore, almost all dogs need to have their nails clipped on a regular basis, at least monthly. This aids in keeping the foot healthy, reduces stress on other joints, and decreases the risk of fractured nails and injured nail beds. Training from puppyhood is important for the dog to be used to having his nails clipped, so that it's not a

Trimming your dog's nails is an important part of his grooming routine.

Check for cracked footpads and swollen areas when cutting your dog's nails.

Regularly cleaning your dog's ears will prevent infections.

major struggle when you attempt to perform this part of the grooming routine.

Several types of clippers specifically designed for canine nails are sold at pet stores and veterinary clinics. Scissor-type clippers can be used on puppies and small breeds. For medium- to large-breed dogs, use guillotine-type clippers. Very large dogs with hard nails may require heavy-duty, pliers-type nail clippers. Hold your dog's foot carefully, pushing down gently at the base of the nail as you snip the tip off. If your dog still has dewclaws, a fifth claw on the inside of the leg, these should be clipped, too.

A significant concern of many owners is cutting a nail too short. If you cut too deeply, you may cut into the nail's blood vessel, which is called the quick. In the event that this happens, it will bleed and inflict momentary pain, but will not be life-threatening in healthy dogs. A styptic stick or other coagulant may be used to stop the bleeding. The easiest way to avoid this is to perform frequent nail clips, cutting off the tips. If nails are allowed to grow long, the vein will grow out as well. However, with regular clipping, the vein in the nail will shrink and the foot will regain its balance.

## Ear Care

Ear cleaning is necessary in many dogs because of the buildup of debris. In order to get rid of dirt and excess wax buildup, ear cleaners are available in pet stores or from a veterinarian. Once or twice a week, cleaning the ear with a suitable pet ear cleaner should suffice for normal dogs. Never use just plain water to clean your dog's ears, because this could lead to an infection; similarly, do not use alcohol or peroxide

Part 3

around the ears. Flush the ear canal with the ear cleaner, massage the base of the ear, and wipe out the excess with a cotton ball.

Some groomers recommend cleaning your dog's ears before each bath. After cleaning the ears and before you wash your dog, insert one or two cotton balls into his ears to make sure no water gets into the ear canal. Be careful never to insert anything including a cotton swab into the dog's ear canal as this could cause ear damage. If your dog has suffered previous ear problems, ask your veterinarian which cleaner he or she recommends.

If excess wax builds up and prevents good air circulation within the ear, infection may develop, causing a foul odor and dark-colored discharge. Redness, excessive debris, and/or foul odors should be addressed by a veterinarian for appropriate treatment, as these are symptoms of an infection. Shaking the head, scratching at the ears, or tilting the head are also signs of ear problems that need veterinary attention. If your dog exhibits these symptoms, he may have allergies, ear mites, or perhaps an aural hematoma (when the blood vessels in the ear flap burst), and you should see your vet immediately.

## Dental Care

The number-one health problem in dogs is periodontal disease. It is also one of the problems that dog owners can easily overlook. Luckily, dental care is becoming more of a routine for most pet owners. Oral hygiene not only keeps canine breath sweet, but it also helps prevent health problems in general. As with our own teeth, the first step in

If your dog is scratching his ears or shaking his head, visit your vet.

Proper oral hygiene keeps your dog's teeth clean.

periodontal disease is plaque (the film that covers the teeth). If not removed with regular brushing, plaque may harden and develop into tartar.

Biscuits, toys, and special diets are marketed to reduce tartar. Biscuits designed to reduce tartar tend to be very hard, thus leading to their effectiveness in removing the debris with abrasion. Hard nylon toys like Nylabones® are structured with many small bumps on the surface to allow more surface contact with the teeth during chewing, sort of a brushing effect. A prescription diet is available from your veterinarian that is specifically manufactured for canines with dental disease.

Brushing your dog's teeth will go a long way toward promoting dental health, and it should be done daily, if possible.

Start by handling the dog's mouth regularly and as early as possible, getting the pet used to fingers and manipulation around the oral cavity. Then dab a small amount of the toothpaste in the mouth to accustom the dog to the flavor. Eventually, the owner may graduate to a toothbrush or gauze pad for actual brushing. Special brushes are available from pet supply stores.

Tartar buildup accumulates with age and may lead to gingivitis or oral diseases. More than 80 percent of dogs by age three have some signs of gum disease. Symptoms of gum disease include bad breath, discolored teeth, red or swollen gums, weight loss, drooling, bloody saliva, and nasal discharge.

Almost all dogs, and some breeds more than others, including Shih Tzus and Pekingese, need regular professional dental cleanings as they age. Bad teeth and gum disease are major sources of infection for the rest of the body, especially

**Doggie Toothpaste**

In order to prevent stomach upsets, only use toothpaste designed for pets. Human toothpaste, baking soda, and salt are not made for brushing your dog's teeth and should not be used.

Chew toys like NYlabones® promote good oral health.

**Part 3**

major organs that include the heart and the kidneys. Feed your dog a nutritious diet, make sure your veterinarian examines your dog's teeth on a regular basis, and provide plenty of chew toys. Keeping your pet's mouth healthy helps keep the whole pet healthy.

## Anal Sacs

Anal sacs are located on each side of the dog's anus. They collect a foul-smelling fluid that the dog may release when excited or fearful or when he's marking his territory. Normally, the fluid is released whenever your dog has a bowel movement. If the drainage of the sacs becomes obstructed, dogs often experience discomfort, such as an itching feeling. Owners may notice their dog sitting on his rear, dragging his bottom by his front feet, or biting the tail area.

Relieving the blockage is an unpleasant task, but it can be done at home by experienced dog owners. However, most owners turn to groomers or veterinary personnel for help, because pet-care professionals know exactly how to express the liquid quickly and easily. If your dog acts like he is in pain when you touch the anal area, you'll need to see a veterinarian. Infections of the sacs require antibiotics for treatment, and in some cases, surgical removal is indicated.

## Coat Care

A healthy dog has a shiny, beautiful coat. Coat care requirements vary greatly, depending on the breed, but brushing and combing your dog's coat regularly is the most important step leading to a well-groomed pet. Short, smooth coats are obviously the easiest to care for properly. Medium and long coats require regular brushing,

Have your dog's teeth checked by the vet at least once a year.

Maintaining your dog's coat will keep it clean and attractive.

Part 3

Brushing your dog's coat helps keep shedding to a minimum.

A pin brush is useful for grooming long-haired breeds.

and you'll spend the most time grooming a long-haired or thick-haired dog. Keeping longer coats in good condition can be time consuming; this is important to consider when choosing a dog. Most full coats may be kept clipped to ease the maintenance. Regular grooming appointments are required to do this.

Length of coat does not directly relate to amount of shedding. Many short-haired breeds shed volumes. There is no such thing as a hypoallergenic breed, but certain breeds do shed very little, such as Poodles. Brushing distributes the dog's skin oils throughout the coat and helps to keep the dog's coat shiny and healthy. It also removes dead hair and skin cells, reducing shedding. Brushing cleans your dog's skin and cuts down on the chance that your dog will contract a skin disease or parasites.

Regular bathing helps to reduce allergen potential. Some dog's coats retain more dirt and need frequent bathing, while other breeds rarely need baths. Dogs may be bathed regularly using safe pet shampoos. Human products are generally too strong for canine skin, so do not use your own shampoo on your pet.

The process of bathing begins with brushing the dry coat to remove dead hair and mats. To prevent soap from irritating the eyes, a small amount of eye lubricant may be used. Cotton balls placed in the ears help prevent water from going inside the canals. Gently place the dog on a rubber mat in the tub. It may be advisable to have an assistant or, at the very least, a collar and leash on the animal to prevent escape. Wet the dog down with warm water using a spray hose. Shampoo may be applied directly to the coat, lathering in well. Some medicated shampoos may need to be left on for five or ten minutes before rinsing. Carefully rinse out all suds thoroughly. The bath process may be

Part 3

# Breed Shedding & Grooming Schedule

| BREED | SHEDDING | GROOMING |
|---|---|---|
| Afghan Hound | some | brush daily |
| Beagle | year round | little |
| Brittany | seasonal | brush weekly |
| Cairn Terrier | seasonal | brush weekly |
| Cocker Spaniel | year round | brush daily |
| Dalmatian | year round | brush weekly |
| Doberman Pinscher | some | little |
| English Springer Spaniel | seasonal | brush 2X a week |
| German Shepherd | lots | brush 3 X a week |
| Greyhound | some | little |
| Siberian Husky | profuse seasonal | brush 2X a week |
| Irish Setter | seasonal | brush 2 X a week |
| Labrador Retriever | seasonal | little |
| Lhasa Apso | minimal | brush daily |
| Maltese | minimal | brush daily |
| Malamute | profuse seasonal | brush 2 X a week |
| Pomeranian | some | brush 2 X a week |
| Pood | very little | clip every 4-6 weeks |
| Rottweiler | some | little |
| Saint Bernard | seasonal | brush twice weekly |
| Shetland Sheepdog | mostly seasonal | brush twice weekly |

Part 3

Whether long- or short-coated, all breeds of dog require regular grooming.

Be careful not to get soap in your dog's eyes when bathing him.

repeated for an especially dirty dog. Gently squeeze the water off legs, tail, ears, and sides. Towel dry, then finish with a blow dryer.

Scratching, redness, sores, scaling, or changes in skin pigment require consultation and treatment by a veterinarian. These symptoms are exhibited by dogs suffering from allergies, skin infections, and external parasites, as well as serious systemic diseases. Accurate diagnosis and therapy depends on the veterinarian and the client working together toward a common goal–a healthy dog.

## Grooming Tools

Consult breed books and professional groomers for types of brushes suitable for your dog, as different breeds require different kinds of grooming tools. For long-coated dogs, a pin brush is useful for regular grooming. A slicker brush removes dead hair on all kinds of breeds, and, for the undercoat, a bristle brush can be used. The bristle brush is useful in grooming shorter coats as well. A rubber brush or curry grooms short, smooth coats. A flea comb is a very fine-toothed comb used to check for fleas and flea debris.

### Pin Brush

The pin brush has rounded smooth tips and is used for regular brushing of long-coated dogs, such as the Lhasa Apso and the Yorkshire Terrier. Pin brushes come in several sizes, with large pins for long-coated, large dogs and small pins for long-coated, small dogs.

### Slicker Brush

The slicker brush removes dead hair and can be used on all kinds of dogs. Heavy varieties of this brush are good at dematting and brushing long-haired breeds, while lighter slicker brushes can be used on short-haired dogs.

## Bristle Brush

The bristle brush is a great all-around brush for everyday grooming. Use this brush on short-haired breeds and also to brush the undercoat of long-haired breeds.

## Grooming Gloves or Mitts

A grooming glove, also known as a hound glove, gets its name from the fact that it works best on short-haired dogs, such as hounds. The brush bristles are embedded into a glove or mitt, which some groomers prefer over holding a brush. A rubber grooming mitt serves much the same purpose as the hound glove.

## Undercoat Rake or Rake Comb

The rake comb removes dead undercoat hair and is best used on coarse-textured or large breeds.

## Combs

There are a number of different types of combs available at pet stores, including fine-toothed, medium-toothed, or wide-toothed. Use a fine-toothed comb on soft, thin, or silky coats. A medium-toothed comb is appropriate for most for average coats, while a wide-toothed comb is best for thick, heavy coats. A matting comb has very wide teeth and is used to help get the tangles out of long-haired coats. Fine-toothed flea combs are helpful at removing fleas from your dog's coat.

A healthy puppy should be strong and sturdy and have a soft, lustrous coat.

Be very gentle when cleaning your dog's ears.

Part 3

A well-groomed appearance begins with good health.

Grooming is an essential part of caring for your dog. If you do not feel comfortable clipping your dog's nails, cleaning his ears, or performing any of the necessary steps listed here, seek out a professional groomer. Veterinary clinics often have groomers on staff, as do many of your better pet stores. A good groomer will not mind if you stop in to ask his or her opinion on what kind of grooming schedule you should follow and will be able to show you the proper way to take care of your dog's nails, ears, and coat.

Part 3

# Your Dog's Health

The cornerstone of preventive veterinary care is regular physical examinations. Your veterinarian should become part of your family's health care team, striving to give your pet a long and healthy life. As a puppy, your pet should be checked regularly at three- to four-week intervals until approximately four months of age. In addition to vaccinations, your veterinarian will be checking for congenital problems such as hernias and heart murmurs, as well as problems that develop as your puppy grows. This allows any disorders to be addressed immediately. Also, your veterinarian is a good source of advice for avoiding behavior problems that may crop up such as chewing or house soiling.

*It's important that you choose the best health care for your pet.*

## Pet Insurance

Statistics show that two out of three pets will experience major medical problems in the course of their lifetime. The high cost of some veterinary procedures, which can run into thousands of dollars, has forced owners that don't have the financial means to make tough decisions: Watch their pet suffer or end its life through euthanasia. To help defray expenses, more and more owners are turning to insurance for their pets. There are several companies throughout the US that offer this type of insurance. Veterinary Pet Insurance (VPI) is the largest, with more than 850,000 clients. It operates just like a traditional human health care insurance plan. Owners can go to any licensed veterinarian, veterinary specialist, or animal hospital in the world. To find out more about pet insurance, ask your veterinarian, call VPI at 800-872-7387, or visit the website at www.veterinarypetinsurance.com.

As an adult dog goes through middle age, annual checkups are necessary to ensure that any problems that arise are noticed and that the appropriate steps are taken. Remember that dogs cannot talk and even if they could, they cannot tell you about a developing heart murmur or small mass in their abdomen. Even observant owners may miss an ear infection, the start of dental disease, or a mild skin inflammation. It is always much easier to take action on a problem early in its course, rather than waiting until it is advanced.

As your dog matures, annual checkups are necessary to ensure good health.

When your dog reaches seven years of age (or five years for giant breeds), annual checkups become even more important. As bodies age, it is more likely that health problems will arise. Annual blood work to check for anemia or kidney, liver, or blood sugar problems may help catch a disease in its early stages. Often, control can be as simple as a diet change. Many owners are fearful of finding out their pet has a problem. An early determination of the dog's problem can make the difference between a high-quality life and chronic

## Correlation of Dog Age to Human Age

Contrary to popular belief, one year in a dog's life does not equal seven years of a human's life. Making the comparison more difficult is the disparity in life spans of different breeds. Small dogs tend to live significantly longer than larger dogs. Giant breeds, such as Newfoundlands, have a relatively short life span of seven to eight years.

| Dog | Human |
|---|---|
| 1 year | 15 years |
| 2 | 24 |
| 3 | 28 |
| 4 | 32 |
| 5 | 36 |
| 6 | 40 |
| 7 | 44 |
| 8 | 48 |
| 9 | 52 |
| 10 | 56 |
| 11 | 60 |
| 12 | 64 |
| 13 | 68 |
| 14 | 72 |
| 15 | 76 |
| 16 | 80 |
| 17 | 84 |
| 18 | 88 |

Do everything you can to ensure that your pet lives a long and rewarding life.

**Part 3**

Diet, exercise, and health care are the three major factors of canine health.

## Life Span of Various Breeds

| | |
|---|---|
| Akita | 10-12 years |
| Boxer | 8-12 |
| Border Collie | 13 |
| Cairn Terrier | 14-16 |
| Chinese Shar-Pei | 7-12 |
| Dalmatian | 11-13 |
| Doberman Pinscher | 10-12 |
| English Springer Spaniel | 12 |
| Golden Retriever | 10-14 |
| Greyhound | 9-14 |
| Irish Setter | 12-14 |
| Keeshond | 12-15 |
| Lhasa Apso | 14 |
| Maltese | 12-15 |
| Alaskan Malamute | 10-12 |
| Pomeranian | 12-17 |
| Pug | 12-14 |
| Rottweiler | 10 |
| Saint Bernard | 8 |
| Scottish Terrier | 12-14 |
| West Highland White Terrier | 12-14 |

illness or death. Geriatric pets of 10 and 11 years and older or even younger animals with previously determined health problems may need more frequent physical examinations, with blood work and urinalysis.

## Spaying and Neutering

Pets generally live longer, healthier lives when spayed (females) or neutered (males). Responsible pet ownership requires that owners avoid indiscriminate breeding of their dogs. Pet overpopulation is a continuing problem in the United States and neutering pets is a path to a solution.

Neutering prevents common problems as male dogs grow older. Castration eliminates the possibility of testicular cancer, as well as reduces the risk of prostate disease and tumors around the rectum. Castration may also limit certain kinds of aggression, making the dog a better family pet. Car accidents and other violent injuries may be reduced, because the male dog's desire to roam will be limited. Female dogs benefit by early spaying to reduce the incidence of breast tumors later on in life. The surgery also eliminates the possibility of developing pyometra, a life-threatening infection of the uterus, and ovarian cancer.

Dogs may be spayed or neutered as early as eight weeks of age. Humane societies are currently performing the surgeries early, in many cases to avoid adopting out an unneutered pet. Most veterinarians prefer to wait until the

Part 3

dog is around five to six months old. For females, it is best performed before the first heat cycle. The spay procedure, technically called an ovariohysterectomy, removes the ovaries, the fallopian tubes, and the uterus through an abdominal incision. The female dog (commonly called a "bitch" in dog circles) will not have heat cycles after surgery. In males, castration (orchiectomy) is the surgical removal of the testicles. Contrary to many owners' fears, dogs do not have an emotional breakdown after surgery. Male dogs do not have the cognizant ability to realize they have been neutered. Most go home happily after surgery to a healthier, safer life.

Most breeders will require that you don't breed your pet-quality puppy.

## Vaccinations

Vaccinating your dog will help protect your pet against various viral and bacterial diseases, some of which can be fatal. Working with your veterinarian is vital to determine your pet's potential exposure to various canine diseases. It is not necessary to vaccinate your dog for every disease that dogs may be inoculated against. Each pet's risk must be assessed individually.

Frequency of vaccinations is a current topic in the veterinary community. Traditionally, most vaccines are boosted annually. Some feel, however, that this may not be necessary. But, until more evidence is collected, vaccine labels should be followed to ensure maximum protection.

### Rabies

A staple of every dog's vaccination protocol should be rabies. All dogs should be protected against this fatal disease. Because rabies can be

Spaying or neutering dogs increases their chances of living healthier lives.

Vaccinations help protect your dog from viral and bacterial diseases.

A fenced-in area protects your dog from parasites.

transmitted to humans, this is a great public health concern. Rabies shots are generally required under the law and are administered every one to three years, depending on the vaccine, the age of the pet, and the area in which you live.

### Canine Distemper

Canine distemper is a highly contagious virus affecting the nervous, gastrointestinal, and respiratory systems. Symptoms may include fever, vomiting, diarrhea, coughing, seizures, and ultimately, death. Some owners fail to vaccinate against distemper due to a misconception surrounding the name of the virus. This disease does not deal with temperament, and protection against it may save your pet's life.

### Parvovirus

Parvovirus is another disease that may lead to your pet's death. Highly contagious, it causes severe vomiting and diarrhea. A second gastrointestinal virus, called corona, may contribute to gastrointestinal illness in dogs. Symptoms are most severe when these viruses are combined. Vaccinations are designed to protect the dog from both diseases. Parvo can be particularly easy for an unprotected canine to contract, as the virus is very strong and can live on inanimate objects for a long period of time.

### Hepatitis, Parainfluenza, and Leptospirosis

Frequently included in vaccinations for distemper and parvovirus are canine hepatitis virus, canine parainfluenza, and canine leptospirosis. Hepatitis is a serious disease that affects primarily the liver, but can also damage your dog's kidneys. Parainfluenza causes a highly contagious cough in dogs. Leptospirosis is a bacterial disease contributing to liver and kidney problems. In addition, leptospirosis causes disease in people.

## Lyme Disease

Lyme disease is an increasing problem in the United States, with more and more cases discovered each year. The Northeast, North Central, and Pacific coast states seem to have the highest incidence of Lyme disease, although it's been reported in 47 states. Vaccination against Lyme disease *(Borreliosis)* has been available for a number of years. As ticks carry this disease, dogs with no exposure to these parasites do not need inoculation. Good tick control programs minimize the necessity for Lyme vaccination. However, dogs with significant exposure should be considered candidates for prevention, as this disease can be devastating to both dogs and humans. Although the deer tick is the best known transmitter of Lyme disease, other types of ticks have been implicated as well. The dog tick can be infected with *Borrelia burgdorferi*. Clinical signs of Lyme disease may include lameness, fever, and lethargy. The bacteria may also affect the heart, kidneys, and even the brain.

## Bordatella

Bordatella inoculation is helpful in boarding situations, as this bacteria is a leading cause of kennel cough, a persistent, hacking cough that is most commonly contracted in kennels. A dog that has no contact with other dogs or is never boarded need not be immunized.

In certain areas, it is wise to vaccinate your dog against Lyme disease.

Clear bright eyes and a shiny coat are signs of good health.

Part 3

*Be sure to check your dog's coat after he has been playing outside.*

### Giardia

A new vaccine is available for protection against infection by giardia. This bacterium is primarily contracted by consumption of contaminated water, causing sudden or chronic diarrhea and leading to debilitation.

### Internal Parasites

There are a number of intestinal parasites that may infect dogs. Puppies may even be born with them or may contract the worms from their mother while nursing. While owners may see certain types of worm pass out in the stool, others are not detectable by this method. Regular microscopic stool checks are needed to determine parasite infestation.

## Vaccination Schedule

| Disease Vaccination (weeks) | Age at 1st Vaccination (weeks) | Age at 2nd Vaccination (weeks) | Age at 3rd Interval (months) | Revaccination |
|---|---|---|---|---|
| Distemper | 6-10 | 10-12 | 14-16 | 12 |
| Canine Hepatitis (CAV-1 or CAV-2) | 6-8 | 10-12 | 14-16 | 12 |
| Parvovirus | 6-8 | 10-12 | 14-16 | 12 |
| Bordetellosis | 6-8 | 10-12 | 14-16 | 12 |
| Parainfluenza | 6-8 | 10-12 | 14-16 | 12 |
| Leptospirosis | 10-12 | 14-16 | — | 12 |
| Rabies | 12 | 64 | — | 12 or 36* |
| Coronavirus | 6-8 | 10-12 | 12-14 | 12 |

*Check with your veterinarian, as this depends on the type of vaccine given.

Part 3

## Roundworms

Roundworms are especially problematic with puppies. Dogs may be born with them, acquire them from nursing, or pick them up from soil contaminated with roundworm eggs. Roundworms are considered zoonotic—meaning they are contagious to people, and children are the most vulnerable. Therefore, many veterinarians recommend prophylactic deworming on puppies to avoid roundworms. Occasionally, owners will notice them when puppies pass long spaghetti-like worms. The eggs may be detected microscopically only.

## Hookworms

Hookworms are also zoonotic. They are passed from the mother to the puppy through the milk or contracted from contaminated soil. This parasite can be very dangerous to young puppies as well as adults, causing bleeding in the gastrointestinal tract. Careful control of hookworm disease is vital for a dog's health.

## Whipworms

Whipworms are yet another parasite that can be problematic for pets. Dogs are infected by contact with contaminated soil. These worms can cause chronic diarrhea. A simple way to control roundworms, hookworms, and whipworms is to place dogs on milbemyein, a monthly heartworm preventative medication that also helps control these internal parasites.

## Tapeworms

Tapeworms are commonly found by owners. They look like small, flat, white grains of rice that appear around the anus or on stools. Dogs

Keeping your yard clean is the best preventative against parasites.

Treating both mother and pups can prevent them from contracting worms.

Part 3

Good health and temperament are passed down from generation to generation.

These two friends share some puppy love.

acquire tapeworms through flea infestation or ingestion of rodents. Effective medication for eradication of tapeworms is available from your veterinarian.

Other internal parasites such as coccidia and giardia may contribute to gastrointestinal problems. These parasites require professional diagnosis and treatment.

### Heartworms

Heartworms, a potentially fatal blood parasite in dogs, are carried by mosquitoes. The parasite settles into the dog's heart, eventually causing symptoms of heart failure. While treatable in most cases, treatment can be expensive and difficult. To save your pet the agony of this disease, a simple blood test may be run to ensure that your dog is not infected. Then, a monthly pill may be given to prevent this disease. Puppies may start their heartworm prevention early and can continue it year round in most areas of the country. After a negative heartworm test, the monthly preventatives available from your veterinarian are safe and effective protection for your dog. Follow your veterinarian's advice for administration of the product.

### External Parasites

Skin parasites are a common problem with dogs, with fleas and ticks being the most common. Fleas are small, cigar-shaped insects that move rapidly across your dog's skin. They may contribute to anemia, parasites, and skin problems. They can also infect the household environment, even being dormant for long periods of time. Flea infestation may be suspected if the owner finds black dirt in the dog's coat while combing. This dirt is actually flea excrement; it bears a strong resemblance to black pepper.

Ticks are relatively flat, oval insects that move slowly. They may be found attached to the dog's skin. Besides contributing to anemia, they carry potentially deadly diseases such as Lyme disease and babesiosis.

There are a number of flea control products currently available. Keep in mind that natural products are not necessarily safe. Effectiveness and safety should both be considered before using any parasite control product.

Another important consideration in any flea control program is to start before flea season begins in your area. Be aware that in some parts of the country, flea season lasts all year long. Be consistent in the application of the product throughout the season.

Remember to be gentle when checking your dog's coat for ticks or fleas.

## Flea & Tick Control

There are a number of effective flea and tick treatments available on the market. Consult your veterinarian, as he or she can help you decide which treatment is best for your canine companion.

Lufenuron is a pill that is administered monthly. This relatively new treatment is basically birth control for fleas. Any fleas that your pet gets will not be able to reproduce. This treatment does not kill adult fleas, but helps control the flea population. It is safe to use in conjunction with flea sprays or other topical agents. All pets in the household must be placed on this product to realize the full effect.

Amitraz is an ingredient present in certain tick collars. It is extremely effective in preventing tick infestations. These collars should be used with caution, as they can be toxic to dogs if chewed or eaten and also can be toxic to children. One method to limit this is to use the collars only when there is exposure to ticks. When the pet is relaxing in the house, put the collar in a sealed plastic bag.

Popular forms of both flea and tick control are pyrethrins and permethrins. These ingredients are available in sprays, topical oils, dips, etc. While they are effective and relatively safe for dogs, they are not the most effective products available today.

Imidacloprid is topical oil for flea control available for monthly use. It kills adult fleas quickly and exposure to it is very safe for both pets and owners. It is the most popular flea control available through veterinarians today.

Fipronil is a flea and tick controller popularly used as topical oil; it is also available as a spray. It is now available over the counter as well as from veterinarians.

Part 3

Keep a watchful eye on your dog when he's outside.

Excessive scratching could indicate a skin allergy.

Ask your veterinarian for advice when to start, as well as which products would be best suited for your pet and your household.

## Other External Parasites

Other external parasites, such as lice and mites, need to be diagnosed and treated by a professional. Ear mites in dogs cause inflammation and may contribute to bacterial or yeast infections. Owners may notice their pet scratching his ears or shaking his head often. As ear infections are more common than ear mites in dogs, a veterinarian should be consulted to determine the cause of your dog's discomfort.

Demodectic mites are microscopic insects that burrow into canine skin. They are not contagious to other dogs or people. Diagnosis is made by the identification of the mite or its eggs microscopically. As there is a hereditary component involving this parasite, dogs diagnosed with it should be neutered. Treatment varies, depending on the extent of skin lesions. Localized patches of demodex, usually found on the head, may be treated locally with a relatively mild salve. More generalized forms of the disease require regular dips with a prescription product after clipping the hair.

Sarcoptic mites cause severe itching in dogs. This parasite may also be identified microscopically, although it can be difficult to track down. Scabies is contagious to humans and other animals, so any suspected case should be treated. When diagnosing the cause of itching in a pet, it is not unusual for a veterinarian to inquire if anyone in the family has a rash.

Other parasites you should be aware of include ringworm and lice. Ringworm is a fungal infection of the skin of dogs. It is not particularly common, but maybe transmitted to people; therefore, professional diagnosis and treatment are in order. Lice may be detected easily using a magnifying glass. Eggs may attach to the hair shaft. Dog lice are not contagious to humans, nor are human lice contagious to dogs.

## Special Health Concerns

### Glaucoma

Glaucoma has been a very frustrating disease for both veterinarians and pet owners. The disease is caused by an increase in intraocular (inside the eye) pressure. This pressure causes changes in the optic nerve and retina early in the disease, sometimes causing permanent blindness within days. Clinical signs seen later in the disease process include conjunctivitis (redness around the eye), corneal edema or gray corneas, scleral and corneal vascularization, and eventually enlargement of the eye to where the eyelids cannot close. Unfortunately, these changes, which will be recognized by dog owners, often are not apparent until permanent blindness has developed. Early detection and treatment are extremely important.

Because your dog cannot complain of headaches or loss of vision, a veterinarian needs to measure the pressure in the dog's eyes annually to detect early changes. The first eye exam will establish a baseline measurement, so that at following checks your veterinarian will know what is normal pressure and what may be abnormal. Your veterinarian can then begin therapy to prevent the inevitable blindness and constant pain of this disease. Check with your breed club to see if occurrences of this problem exist to a

Petting gives you the chance to keep on top of your dog's physical condition.

Maintaining your dog's health includes annual veterinary checkups.

Part 3

Responsible pet owners are aware of breed-specific health concerns.

degree that dictates seeking a veterinarian's adice.

## Clotting Disorders

Besides glaucoma, there are several clotting disorders to which many dog breeds are predisposed. This is especially important to screen for before surgery. There is a simple blood test that your veterinarian should be able to perform in the office. Check with your breed club to see if occurrences of this problem exist to a degree that dictates seeking a veterinarian's advice.

Part 3

# Home Treatments and First Aid

## Treating Illness

Dogs may develop minor illnesses that are easily managed at home. Chief among these are vomiting and diarrhea, often due to the canines indiscriminate appetite.

### Vomiting

For vomiting, the owner should supply water in small sips or ice chips. You may also give amounts of an electrolyte solution (like a sports drink). No food should be offered for 12 to 24 hours. Profuse vomiting or symptoms that last longer than one day require a visit to the veterinarian.

Choosing a reputable, caring vet will help your pet to feel more comfortable.

If your dog seems unusually lethargic, consult your veterinarian.

Having a basic knowledge of first aid could help save your pet's life.

### Diarrhea

Home treatment of diarrhea includes resting the bowels, with no food for 12 to 24 hours. An antidiarrheal may be given at 1 teaspoon per 25 pounds every four to six hours. A weak pet with profuse or bloody diarrhea needs professional treatment. Minor cases should clear up within a day or two.

### Allergic Reactions

Allergic reactions, like hives, may be treated at home. Symptoms include facial swelling and visible welts over the body. An antihistamine is effective in many cases. Breathing should be carefully observed.

### Sore Legs

Many dogs suffer from sore legs due to muscle injury or arthritis. Most respond well to a buffered aspirin given 1/2-1 per 25 pounds of dog every 12 hours. If the lameness is severe or chronic, a veterinarian should be consulted.

Aspirin may upset the canine stomach and should be discontinued if the dog vomits or stops eating. Chronic arthritis may be helped by nutritional supplements containing glucasamine, chondroitin sulfate, and perna canaliculus mussels. There are a number of products on the market available at pet stores and your veterinarian's office.

### Emergency First Aid

Whenever you're handling an injured dog, it's advisable to restrain the animal. Even the most beloved canine best friend can turn and bite his owner if he is frantic or in pain. The easiest way

Part 3

to restrain a dog is to use a muzzle. Simple household items such as a necktie or short piece of rope can be knotted to make a temporary muzzle. Make sure your make-do muzzle does not interfere with the dog's breathing, but is tight enough to prevent him from slipping loose.

## Heatstroke

Canine heatstroke victims should be immediately cooled in a tub of running cool water or with a bath of running cool water from a hose. Placing the dog in front of an electric fan will help dissipate the heat more quickly. Ice packs may be applied to the groin and neck areas. If the dog does not recover in short order, a trip to the veterinarian is needed to prevent permanent injury or death. The wet dog should be transported in the car with the windows down so as to utilize the air current and aid in cooling.

## Cuts

Cuts occur most frequently on paws or legs. Some can be prevented by the owner carefully inspecting the areas where the dog romps for glass, cans, or sharp rocks. Water can contain hidden dangers. Putting persistent, direct pressure on the wound for five minutes may stem bleeding. Ice packs help reduce swelling. If blood is spurting in a strong geyser-like fashion, an artery may have been damaged and immediate veterinary care is indicated.

If the blood flow is not profuse, the wound may be cleaned and evaluated for the need of

It's best to keep your dog cool and relaxed in hot weather.

Unusual behavior could be an indication that your puppy doesn't feel well.

A leash helps keep your dog safe when he is outside of the home.

Maintaining your dog's immunization schedule will increase the longevity of his life.

sutures. Most small wounds will heal adequately on their own if kept clean with peroxide and treated with antibiotic ointment (such as bacitracin). Dogs must not be allowed to lick their wounds, as this may delay healing.

Fights with other dogs may inflict serious puncture wounds. These wounds can be deceiving, exhibiting only small holes on the surface of the skin, but hiding damage beneath. If the dog is bright, alert, active, and eating, veterinary care may be delayed for up to one day if the owner carefully cleans the wounds. Dogs that are depressed or lethargic, with swelling around the lesions, need immediate care. Drainage and exploration of the wounds are in order. Antibiotics are almost always needed for puncture wounds.

## Car Accidents

The best control is a well-trained dog and a leash, but sometimes car accidents happen. If a pet is hit by a car, the results can be devastating. All dogs, even ones that seem fine, need to be evaluated after a car accident. The veterinarian will check for normal bladder function, difficulty breathing, and gums that are a normal pink color. While broken legs are generally not life-threatening, shock and internal injuries may lead to death. A dog lying on the ground, eyes glassy and breathing shallowly, may be in shock and should immediately be taken to a veterinarian. A severely injured dog may be transported to a veterinary hospital after carefully tying his mouth shut and using a blanket as a stretcher. Carry the dog gently, as internal injuries can be worsened with rough handling.

## Poisons

Dogs have a voracious appetite that can easily get

them into trouble. Many items commonly found on a homeowner's property can be toxic to dogs. Antifreeze ingestion leads to kidney failure. Rodent poisons may cause life-threatening hemorrhage for up to one month after ingestion. Even chocolate may be toxic if consumed in a large quantity.

Noncaustic poisons must be addressed immediately by inducing the pet to vomit. To do this, place a small amount of dry mustard or salt on the back of the tongue. You can also administer syrup of ipecac or hydrogen peroxide orally. If you suspect your dog has gotten into a poisonous substance, it is critical that you find exactly what poison he has ingested, so you can tell the veterinarian. Try to determine how much the dog ate or drank.

Cleaning out your dog's eyes should be a part of his daily grooming.

### First Aid Kits

All homes with pets should have a first aid kit. You can purchase a pet first aid kit at your veterinarian's office or your local pet store, or you can create one on your own. A basic kit can be simple, but should have certain staple ingredients.

**NAPCC**

The ASPCA National Poison Center is available 24 hours a day at 1-888-426-4435 or at 1-900-680-0000.

First, you need a rectal thermometer; feeling your dog's nose is not an accurate method of determining a fever. To use, lubricate the tip and gently insert into the rectum.

You'll need a good wound cleaner, such as chlorhexiderm or hydrogen peroxide. For wound treatment, an antibiotic ointment is good. A couple of gauze squares and some bandages round out the wound treatment materials. A pair of scissors may be useful when you cannot take the time to dig for a household pair, as will tweezers.

Part 3

Eyewash comes in handy to flush out debris or clean up an injured eye. Saline solution used by contact lens wearers may also be used. An antihistamine may be used for an allergic reaction or vomiting. An antidiarrheal may be useful. Be sure to ask your veterinarian for a specific dosage recommendation, as doses should be tailored to your pet's specific needs.

*A healthy dog should be playful, outgoing, and happy.*

## First Aid Kit

Before you bring your puppy home, you should put together a first aid kit, which should include:

- Vital information card which includes name, address and phone number of your vet; name, address and phone number of the nearest 24-hour emergency veterinary clinic; and the number of the National Animal Poison Control Center.

- A muzzle, pantyhose, or stretchable gauze that could make a muzzle.

- Scissors

- Tweezers

- Eyewash

- Antibiotic ointment or powder

- Hydrogen peroxide

- Milk of Magnesia

- Thermometer

- K-Y Jelly

- Gauze rolls

- Adhesive bandaging tape

- Cotton balls

- Antibacterial soap

- Blanket or towels

- Rubbing alcohol

Buffered aspirin will relieve minor aches and pains. Note that you should make sure it's buffered aspirin only—not coated, not ibuprofen, and not one of the myriad other over-the-counter medicines available for people. Dogs' stomachs are prone to ulcers. These other pain drugs may cause life-threatening gastric bleeding and should only be used under a veterinarian's supervision. Also note that buffered aspirin can be toxic to cats.

Last, print your veterinarian's telephone number on an index card and keep it inside the kit. If your veterinarian also provides an emergency weekend or relief veterinarian's phone number, add this, too. When you're in an emergency situation, you don't want to be scrambling for a phone book or trying to remember which phone number to call from memory.

*Any dog, regardless of breed, is capable of becoming a lifelong companion.*

Accidents happen. By being prepared with a first aid kit and the knowledge of what to do in an emergency situation, you'll be ready for whatever comes along. Hopefully, your preparations will keep minor accidents from turning into major situations.

**Part 3**

## General Information

**American Kennel Club**

5580 Centerview Drive

Raleigh, NC 27606

919-233-9767

http://www.akc.org


**United Kennel Club**

100 E. Kilgore Road

Kalamazoo, MI 49001

616-343-9020

http://www.ukcdogs.com


**Canadian Kennel Club**

Commerce Park

89 Skyway Avenue, Suite 100

Etobicoke, Ontario M9W 6R4


**The Kennel Club**

1-5 Clarges Street

Piccadilly, London W1Y 8 AB

United Kingdom

www.the-kennel-club.org.uk


**American Society for the Prevention of Cruelty to Animals**

424 East 92nd Street

New York, NY 10128-6804

www.aspca.org


**The Humane Society of the United States**

2100 L Street NW

Washington, DC 20037

# Training and Activities

**Association of Pet Dog Trainers (APDT)**

17000 Commerce Parkway

Suite C

Mt Laurel, NJ 08054

800-PET-DOGS

E-Mail: information@apdt.com

**National Association of Dog Obedience Instructors (NADOI)**

2286 East Steel Road

St. Johns, MI 48879

**American Dog Trainers' Network**

161 West 4th Street

New York, NY 10014

212-727-7257

**North American Flyball Association, Inc.**

1002 E. Samuel Avenue

Peoria Heights, IL 61614

www.flyball.org

**US Dog Agility Association, Inc.**

PO Box 850955

Richardson, TX 75085-0955

972-487-2200

www.usdaa.com

**Alpo Canine Frisbee™ Disc Championships**

(888) 444-ALPO

www.alpo.com

**Canine Freestyle Federation**

Monica Patty, Corresponding Secretary

21900 Foxden Lane

Leesburg, VA 20175

www.canine-freestyle.org

**Musical Canine Sports International**

c/o Val Culpin

3466 Creston Drive

Abbotsford, British Columbia

Canada V2T 5BF9

www.dog-play.com/musical.htm

**United Schutzhund Clubs of America**

3810 Paule Avenue

St. Louis, MO 63125-1718

314-638-9686

www.germanshepherddog.com

E-mail: USASchutzhund@worldnet.att.net

**Therapy Dogs International, Inc.**

88 Bartley Road

Flanders, NJ 07836

(973) 252-9800

tdi-dog.org/training.htm

**Delta Society**

289 Perimeter Road East

Renton, WA 98055-1329

(425) 226-7357

www.deltasociety.org

# Travel

## US Accommodations Catalog

The Automobile Association of America (AAA)

(800) 222-4357

www.aaa.com

Lists accommodations throughout the US. Most places indicate if they accept dogs.

## Vacationing with Your Pet Guide

Pet-Friendly Publications

2327 Ward Road

Pocomoke City, MD 28851

Lists approximately 25,000 hotels and motels that accept pets throughout the United States and Canada. It is published by and available through most bookstores.

## American Boarding Kennels Association

Tel. (719) 591-1113

www.abka.com

## National Association of Professional Pet Sitters

1200 G Street, NW

Suite 760

Washington, DC 20005

(800) 296-7387

www.petsitters.org

## Pet Sitters International

418 East King Street

King, NC 27021

(800) 268-7487

www.petsit.com

# Health

## Veterinary Pet Insurance (VPI)

800-872-7387

www.veterinarypetinsurance.com.

## The National Animal Poison Control Center (NAPCC)

1-800-548-2423 charged $30.00 per case on credit card, no charge for follow up calls, or call 1-900-680-0000, charge $20.00 for five minutes, plus $2.95 for each additional minute---no follow up.

## The Orthopedic Foundation for Animals (OFA)

2300 E Nifong Blvd.

Columbia, MO 65201

573-442-0418

www.offa.org

## Institute for Genetic Disease Control in Animals

PO Box 222

Davis, CA 95617

## The Canine Eye Registration Foundation (CERF)

Department of Veterinary Clinical Science

SChool of Veterinary Medicine

Perdue University

West Lafayette, IN 47907

317-494-8179

www.prodogs.com

# Index

Photo Credits

**Paulette Braun:** p. 27; p. 33; p. 45, top; p. 122; p. 123; p. 151, bottom; p. 160, bottom.

**Isabelle Francais:** p. 9 through p. 26; p. 28, p. 29; p. 30; p. 35 through p. 44; p. 45, bottom; p. 46 through p. 111; p. 114 through p. 121; p. 124; p. 125; p. 126; p. 127; p. 128; p. 130 through p. 150; p. 151, top; p. 152 through p. 159; p. 161 through p.183.

**Alice Pantfoeder:** p. 111; p. 112; p. 113.

**Karen Taylor:** p. 34; p.67; p. 129.

Cartoons by **Michael Pifer**